D756.5 .N6 B75 2004b
Brinkley, Douglas.
Voices of valor

D0771315

Colorado Mountain College
Quigley Library
3000 County Road 114
Glenwood Springs, CO

THE FINAL OVERLORD PLAN

DROP ZONES
D DAY PHASE LINE

5   10

FIRST   SECOND
U.S.   Br

DA

V

30

1

29(-)

1(+)

50

3 Cdn

3

6(-)

Pointe du Hoe

amp-les Bains
Vierville-sur-Mer
St Laurent-sur-Mer   Colleville-sur-Mer

OMAHA

Arromanches-
les Bains   GOLD

JUNO

Trévières   Port-en-Bessin

Aure R.

Courseulles-
sur-Mer

SWORD

Lion-
sur-Mer

Cabourg

E   S   S
BAYEUX   Seulles R.

Ouistre-
ham

Forêt de
Cerisy

Orne R.

St
Manvieu

CAEN

Troarn

Divès R.

Bourguébus

Vimont

VOICES OF VALOR

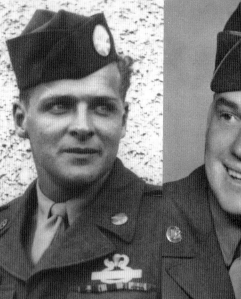

VOICES OF VALOR

D–DAY: JUNE 6, 1944

**DOUGLAS BRINKLEY AND
RONALD J. DREZ**

KONECKY&KONECKY

Konecky & Konecky
72 Ayers Point Rd.
Old Saybrook, CT 06475

Copyright © 2004 by Douglas Brinkley and Ronald J. Drez

Audio (enclosed CDs) © 2004 by the Eisenhower Center for American Studies at the University of New Orleans. These recordings are included courtesy of the Peter S. Kalikow World War II Oral History Project at the Eisenhower Center for American Studies at the University of New Orleans.

Narration copyright © 2004 by Stephen Lang

10 digit ISBN 1-56852-691-1
13 digit ISBN: 978-1-56852-691-1

All rights reserved. No part of this book may be reproduced in any form or by any electronic or mechanical means, including information storage and retrieval systems, without permission in writing from the publisher, except by a reviewer who may quote brief passages in a review.

This edition published by special arrangement with Bulfinch Press, New York, NY.

Voices of Valor: D-Day: June 6, 1944 is produced by becker&mayer!, Bellevue, Washington. www.beckermayer.com

Design by Todd Bates

Printed and bound in Korea

To Peter S. Kalikow,
whose generosity and patriotism have allowed the voices of the men of D-Day to be
preserved for posterity.

CONTENTS

INTRODUCTION

When director Steven Spielberg was a teenager, he had a chance encounter with his hero, the legendary John Ford. "Out of all your movies, which are you most proud of?" the aspiring filmmaker asked the aging icon—to which Ford replied without a beat: "*D-Day*, son. But it hasn't been made yet." Ford had been in charge of a U.S. Signal Corps camera unit on Omaha Beach on June 6, 1944, his mission to film the Operation Overlord invasion that landed 176,000 Allied soldiers on the beaches of Normandy for a massive assault against the Germans occupying France. Somehow, however, Ford's footage was lost until 1998, when Melvin R. Paisley, a World War II aviator and Reagan-era Assistant Secretary of the Navy, found a few canisters of the missing film deep within the National Archives. Spielberg—whose father had also served in the U.S. Army Air Corps, and who was about to win the Best Director Oscar for his D-Day movie *Saving Private Ryan*—was intrigued when he read about Paisley's find in an article historian Douglas Brinkley wrote in *The New Yorker.*

OPPOSITE: American troops at an English port wait to embark on their crossing to Normandy.

But Spielberg had already made his own epic movie, which, along with four recent Stephen E. Ambrose books—*Band of Brothers: E Company, 506th Regiment, 101st Airborne from Normandy to Hitler's Eagle Nest* (1991), *D-Day: June 6: 1944: The Climactic Battle of World War II* (1994), *Pegasus Bridge: June 6, 1944* (1988), and *Citizen Soldiers: The U.S. Army from the Normandy Beaches to the Bulge to the Surrender of Germany, June 7, 1944 to May 7, 1945* (1997)—reignited public interest in what had transpired across the Atlantic on June 6, 1944. "*Saving Private Ryan* will always have a special place in my life because I, too, am surrounded by veterans who—recognizing me at a movie theater or even at a car wash—want to talk about what our film did to unearth many of their hidden memories and now they can tell someone about it," Spielberg wrote to Ambrose on March 30, 1999. "When our national psyche focuses on every bit of faddish trivia, ignoring the greatest event of the twentieth century, D-Day, of course it makes sense that those individuals would not feel welcome to speak and now they are welcome. I am very proud of that and very proud of you for taking a bit of the fire from the torch that you've been carrying for 40 years, and lending it to me this year."

D-Day was the turning point of World War II. There were certainly other pivotal moments: moments when great battles were won or important decisions made. But in sheer magnitude of accomplishments nothing compared to D-Day. British prime minister Winston Churchill summed it up best when he deemed it "the most difficult and most complicated operation ever to take place." That is saying a lot. For it was a rare day during the war when something crucial didn't transpire somewhere in the Pacific, Burma-India-China, the Middle East, North Africa, the Soviet Union, the North Atlantic, or Europe. On June 4, 1944, for example, the Americans marched triumphantly into Rome, the first major capital to be liberated by the Allies. But Italy had started the war as one of the Axis powers, on the side of Fascism in general and Adolf Hitler in particular. With the D-Day invasion in northern France two days after the liberation of Rome, there was a turning point of a different sort: land conquered by the Nazis was taken back for freedom. It was only a narrow strip of sea-sprayed beach, but it was land, hard-fought for, and it was the beginning of the end for Adolf Hitler. "In the column I want to tell you what the opening of the second front entailed," *Stars and Stripes'* Ernie Pyle wrote shortly after D-Day, "so that you can know and appreciate and forever be humbly grateful to those both dead and alive who did it for you."

Everything about D-Day was large—the overarching strategy, the vast mobilization, the sheer number of troops. But it's the daring boldness and intrepid courage of the men—America's 1st, 4th, and 29th Infantry Divisions, and its 82nd and 101st Airborne Divisions, along with the British 3rd and 50th Infantry Divisions, the Canadian 3rd Infantry Division, and the British 6th Airborne Division—plus the incredible job of the U.S. Navy and Air Corps, that stand out. One can read biographies of Dwight Eisenhower or watch footage of John Ford, but the only way to understand D-Day fully is as a battle at its smallest: that is, one soldier and one reminiscence at a time. Collectively these fighting men were the *Voices of Valor*—the title of this book. Infantryman Al Littke of the 16th Regiment Combat Team, for example, watched the naval bombardment of Omaha Beach as he waited in a boat to join the landing. "With all this fire power, it should be a cinch," he recalled saying to himself, "I thought I was untouchable." Leonard Griffing was a paratrooper with the 101st Airborne Division, preparing to drop onto French soil from a low-flying airplane. "As I stood there with my hands on the edge of the doorway ready to push out," he recalled, "it seemed that we took some kind of a burst under the left wing because the plane went in a sharp roll and I couldn't push myself out because it was uphill, so I just hung on."

D-Day was not one day, but a composite of many days, experienced by each of those individuals who played a part on the Allied side—from the 120,000 men who landed during the initial action to the millions of personnel who supported them. In this volume, the story of D-Day is told through the impressions of those who were there. None of the people who lend their voices here saw the grand sweep of the battle, but rather only one small snapshot of it. Assembled in this book, *Voices of Valor*, are those memories—some tragic, some humorous, and all of them imbued with human drama. They comprise the big picture of the largest invasion force ever assembled.

Essentially, this book was born in 1983 when the then director of the Eisenhower Center at the University of New Orleans, historian Stephen E. Ambrose, started interviewing D-Day veterans for an oral history project. Realizing how extraordinary it would have been to have had the technology to tape-record the soldiers of Gettysburg or Vicksburg during the U.S. Civil War, Ambrose and his associate, Captain Ron Drez, USMC, a rifle company commander in Vietnam in 1968, embarked on a mission. For over a decade they canvassed America, attending veterans reunions and tracking down forgotten men. The Eisenhower Center collection, due to the hard work of Ambrose and Drez, eventually grew to more than 2,000 accounts of personal D-Day experiences. "This is the most extensive first-person, I-was-there collection of memoirs of a single battle in existence," Ambrose wrote in the "Acknowledgments" to his best-selling book *D-Day: June 6, 1944: The Climactic Battle of World War II*. "Although space limitations made it impossible for me to quote directly from each oral history or written memoir, all the accounts contributed to my understanding of what happened."

This extraordinary collection of oral histories, which the National D-Day Museum in New Orleans now curates, formed the basis of Ambrose's four seminal World War II books. What Ambrose learned was that those veterans were reluctant storytellers—but great ones. Leonard G. Lomell, of the 2nd Ranger Battalion, spoke for what Tom Brokaw has dubbed "The Greatest Generation," when in typically self-deprecating fashion, he explained the rationale of most D-Day veterans. "We didn't write articles, books, make speeches or publicize the performance of our duties," he admitted. "We know what each other did and we did our duty like professionals. We weren't heroes, we were just good Rangers as we believed the record would forever show."

The record, as offered in this volume, does indeed show that they didn't just do their job "well"—they were magnificent. With the financial help of Peter S. Kalikow, president of one of New York City's leading real estate firms, the Eisenhower Center is continuing to preserve the voices and stories of the men and women who participated in World War II. Besides oral history recordings, the Center has collected written memoirs, letters, photographs, and other documents from veterans and their families. The Center has also worked in conjunction with Encyclopedia Britannica in the creation of its Normandy website, and is now contributing content to military.com for its World War II history page, based on the Center's oral history collection, a sampling of which constitutes this book.

The expression "D-Day" was not coined for the Allied invasion. The same name was given to the undesignated attack date of nearly every planned offensive during the war. It was first coined during World War I, before the massive American attack on Saint Mihiel; the "D" was short for *day*. Albeit redundant, the expression stood for "Day-day." By the end of World War II, though, it stood for only one date: June 6, 1944. That date was utterly unknown when planning for D-Day started in 1943. The first thoughts about it, however, had started long before that. In Washington, it started in 1942 when American diplomats worried that with the Axis powers already occupying most of the European continent, the Soviet Union could be the next to fall. Adding to the anxiety was the fact that the Nazis had been notching one victory after another on the eastern front. Even as the ferocious Battle of Stalingrad raged in late 1942, U.S. officials pressured the British to prepare for an invasion of Occupied France. The ulterior motive, of course, was to siphon German military strength away from the U.S.S.R. Reluctantly, the British agreed to a plan called Operation Roundup, scheduled for 1943, but they soon managed to shift the Allied imperative to North African operations and the eventual invasion of Italy from the Mediterranean.

The Allied victory in North Africa delayed the D-Day invasion in France by a year, and affected it in another way, as well. Field Marshal Erwin Rommel, the respected strategist known as the "Desert Fox," had lost North Africa, but in Germany was nonetheless regarded as a hero. Temporarily out of work, thanks to the Allies, Rommel was ordered to inspect fortifications along the Atlantic coast from the French border with Spain to the Dutch border with Germany: the defense installation known as the Atlantic Wall. The Nazis were well aware that the Allies were considering an invasion across the English Channel, so Rommel was soon given direct responsibility for defending northern France, Belgium, and Holland against an Allied landing. It was a job better suited to a spider, who would spin a web and wait for prey, than to a fox, at his best on the move. Rommel diligently made improvements to fortifications along the coast, though, and tried to anticipate the Allies' next move.

DOUGLAS BRINKLEY AND RONALD J. DREZ

Until the spring of 1943, the Allies were not at all sure themselves just when Roundup might re-emerge, though an effective planning team under a savvy Briton, Lieutenant General Sir Frederick E. Morgan, started analyzing possibilities in March. In the meantime, the United States continued to press its impatience upon the British. But not through diplomacy. Through massive deployment. By June 1943, German U-boats had withdrawn from the offensive in the North Atlantic, and after that, the sea lane was largely safe for the flow of materiel from the U.S. "Arsenal of Democracy" to supply depots throughout Great Britain. From certain angles, Britain seemed to be one large staging area, with tanks lined up in rows literally by the mile, and fighter planes disappearing into the distance like some sort of abstract painting. D-Day was obviously coming, but it awaited a firm plan and the commanders to carry it out.

Finally, in late November 1943, a course was set. In the swirl of the diplomatic meetings that preceded the conference for Allied leaders at Tehran, the British finally concurred

Assault troops line up for supplies and provisions before their departure from England to Normandy.

with the Soviets and the Americans that the time had come to plan an invasion. A D-Day offensive in Europe had become an imperative. At Tehran, President Franklin Roosevelt, Marshal Joseph Stalin, and Prime Minister Winston Churchill formally agreed to go on the offensive on the western front. "The history of war does not know of an undertaking comparable to it for breadth of conception, grandeur of scale, and mastery of execution," Stalin claimed. At the time, the western front lay somewhere in the middle of the English Channel. The strategy had to encompass two major challenges: to cross some hundred miles of open water with a vast army and simultaneously to fight a battle on a scale never attempted before.

Just hearing Churchill agree to attempt the invasion wasn't enough for the Soviets. The British had been evasive before, but at Tehran an impatient Stalin decided to lock in the decision by demanding to know two things: when and who. The question of when was left up to Churchill, whose natural reflex was delay on the matter of the invasion. His reticence was somewhat understandable. Defeat would have left his homeland vulnerable to counterattack: another Battle of Britain. However, he responded to Stalin at Tehran by confirming that the invasion would take place in spring of 1944. With the time frame set, the question of who would command the operation was next. The United States, which would have the most troops in the invasion force, was accorded the privilege of naming the Supreme Commander. Initially, Franklin Roosevelt was inclined to name George C. Marshall, his chief of staff, but in truth, he needed Marshall too much in Washington. Winston Churchill's own choice was General Dwight D. Eisenhower. Ultimately, he was the man Roosevelt selected.

Eisenhower, born in Texas and raised in Kansas, was a colonel when America entered World War II. Despite his relatively low rank, he was already marked for an important role in the war. An energetic man widely recognized for his meticulous tactical ability, Eisenhower was also innately diplomatic. In his dealings with superiors and subordinates alike, he was remarkably adaptable—a quality not often ascribed to ranking military officers. He judged situations, as well as people, individually. Famous for his contagious smile, he could dominate a room as easily with his cogent grasp of detail as with his withering blue-eyed glare. At this time, General Eisenhower had developed three maxims to live by: a) "Never send a battalion to take a hill if you have a division available"; b) "Long faces never win wars"; and c) "The art of leadership is deciding what to do, and then getting men to *want* to do it."

In charge of the buildup in Britain starting in 1942 and the Allied operations in North Africa in 1943, Eisenhower worked closely with officers throughout the Allied chain of command. Though most of them were surprised that General Marshall had not been chosen to execute the invasion, none doubted Eisenhower's ability to handle the job.

To plan the operation, given the name Overlord, Eisenhower depended on a staff of fourteen thousand people, hand-picking as many of them as possible. General Morgan and most of his original staff were retained. The new effort started up where Morgan's had left off, eventually expanding the scope of the planned invasion. Meanwhile, during the winter of 1943, Allied troops were still pouring into Britain. The majority of them were Americans. A holiday atmosphere settled over the British homefront, a sense that it was a time like no other: rambunctious early on, it grew more somber as the weeks went by. No one outside Eisenhower's inner circle knew quite what shape D-Day would take, but everyone knew that it would be big and that it was drawing near. By late April, an incredible 2,876,000 troops were encamped in England, sometimes in tents, sometimes in people's living rooms. By the end of May, that number would rise to well over three million. With them were more than five thousand ships and landing craft, three thousand aircraft, and all of the accoutrements to keep machines and men running at peak performance.

Included in the list of items requisitioned for Overlord were empty ammunition boxes, paper tents, and cloth fighter planes, and they arrived just as ordered. Deception was a crucial part of the planning for D-Day. Even General George C. Patton, one of the U.S. Army's most aggressive officers, became a cardboard general for the sake of D-Day, setting up a camp in southeastern England apparently crammed with troops and pointed at a crossing into Pas-de-Calais. The camp was only part of the deception.

The Pas de Calais, French for the Strait of Dover, was a logical choice for a channel crossing. The shortest distance between England and France, at about twenty-five miles, it was the span favored for decades by intrepid swimmers. Across the Strait, the French *départemente* of Pas-de-Calais was also the most heavily fortified spot along the Atlantic Wall, home to three German fortresses. That was no secret to the Allies because it was no secret to the French Resistance fighters—civilians who spied on the Germans out of half-opened eyes and then found ways of transmitting their information to Paris, where it was sent by radio to the Allies.

Eisenhower's planners were directing their real ships, their airplanes, and their deadly ammo at another landing entirely. They chose the sandy beaches of Normandy, between two deep-port cities: Cherbourg, on the tip of a blunted peninsula, and Le Havre, about one hundred miles to the east. Each of those ports was defended by a German fortress, but the long crescent between was less heavily fortified. It looked out on one of the widest points in the Channel, as much as one hundred miles across, which is why the Nazis presumed it to be relatively safe from attack. That is not to say, however, that it was free for the taking.

The land looking out on the Channel was crisscrossed with barricades and gun installations, and practically paved with land mines. In addition, the Germans had positioned several first-rate gun batteries along the Normandy beaches, the largest of them equipped with 8-inch guns. The water itself was also fortified, with both submerged mines and even more daunting ones on the ends of poles set at a slant to intercept incoming boats. The fortifications were buttressed by tanks, and all of that only constituted the first line of defense. The second line, however, was something of a roving proposition. To make the best use of a limited number of armored vehicles, the Germans had finally settled on a plan to leave the mass of tanks well behind the lines, ready to rush to the defense of any sector under attack. Air power was also stretched thin, but 650 planes were stationed in northern France.

German forces were outmatched in numbers, but they could still easily effect a victory and quash an Allied landing. In the months leading up to D-Day, General Eisenhower sought to increase his advantage by pulling bombers from missions over Germany and redirecting them to strike intermediate targets, especially supply lines, to choke the defenses at Normandy. It was one of the many controversial decisions that he made before D-Day. It was an unpopular one, especially with those in the Air Corps who believed that total victory grew demonstrably closer with every air strike on German soil. Eisenhower's strategy worked, though, in paving the way for the invasion. When the invasion started, there was a four-day backup on the railroad lines leading into the region.

The target of the D-Day invaders was a sixty-mile stretch of shoreline in the middle of the Cherbourg–Le Havre crescent. In places, it offered smooth beaches, with fairly empty farmland beyond. In other places, a narrow strip of sand was buttressed by cliffs ranging from ten to one hundred feet high. The Allies separated their assault into five amphibious divisions and gave names to the beaches where each one would land. Those names have become hallowed: Utah, Omaha, Gold, Juno, and Sword.

While the Germans rearranged panzers and personnel to meet the expected attack (by Patton's army) at Pas-de-Calais, millions of Allies were quietly preparing for the move on Normandy. It was the biggest secret of the war, and, amazingly, the Germans never heard anything about it. As Eisenhower wrote to the Combined Chiefs of Staff on the upcoming Operation Overlord on January 23, 1944: "Every obstacle must be overcome, every inconvenience suffered, and every risk run to ensure that our blow is decisive. We cannot afford to fail."

The Allies knew precisely where they were going. But they had little control over when. The skies had to be clear and the seas calm. Neither proved to be the case during the first few days of June, when all else was ready. Eisenhower was forced by weather conditions to withhold the order to start the invasion. Finally, the conditions began to clear. Though there was no guarantee on the weather, Eisenhower had to take the risk. With every other detail masterminded, he had to revert to sheer hope and trust in the forecasts of his weathermen. Fortunately, their predictions were accurate.

On June 4 Eisenhower gave the Order of the Day: "Good Luck! And let us all beseech the blessing of Almighty God upon this great and noble undertaking." On the night of June 5, the operation finally began, as Allied paratroopers boarded planes and gliders. "OK, let's go" was Eisenhower's direct order. Just after midnight, June 6, they began landing behind enemy lines, with orders to attack and destroy German gun batteries. The success of the paratroopers was instrumental in deciding the fate of the landing force in various sectors. Meanwhile, an armada of ships started making its way toward the designated beaches. Transport vessels were loaded with 125,000 soldiers, on whom the Allied cause depended. At dawn, the navy launched a brutal barrage on the targeted areas. It was soon joined by an air attack of equal ferocity. The sky, just growing light in the early morning, was darkened by an awesome canopy of 2,219 warplanes. The naval assault came from a fleet just as impressive, consisting of six battleships, two monitors, twenty-two cruisers, and sixty-three destroyers—all blasting away at a stretch of beach only two dozen miles long. Up to that point, everything in Overlord was going according to plan.

Even the theatrics worked—much better than expected. Using decoys and a smattering of airplanes towing kite tails of tin foil, carefully designed to attract the attention of German radar, the Allies convinced Nazi commanders that a massive invasion had begun—at Pas-de-Calais. Even reports of the paratrooper activity behind the Normandy beach lines failed to dissuade the Germans. On the contrary, they concluded that the *paratroopers* were the decoys, deployed to draw German forces away from Pas-de-Calais and to the beaches of Normandy.

Allied troops began landing at 6:30 a.m. Wading through the water onto French soil, they met vastly different fates. At Utah Beach, the farthest west, bombardments had decimated the German defenses. Moreover, an opportune navigational mistake had landed the troops at a practically unguarded stretch of the beach. The Americans who landed at Utah sustained relatively few casualties. The British and Canadian forces who landed at Gold and Juno beaches fought their way ashore, according to plan, and were soon followed by tanks, the mere sight of which swept most of the German resistance away. The young soldiers stationed to defend that part of the beach were just not expecting to see tanks emerge from the ocean. The fighting was harder at Sword Beach, the easternmost invasion site, where German defenders stiffened against the specter of the Allies capturing the nearby city of Caen, an important rail depot.

Even at midday, with all that was happening, the German leaders still wouldn't release reserve forces for the defense of the Normandy beaches. Commanders insisted that they would not be fooled. But they were.

For all of the tragedies, the blunders, and the strokes of luck, good and bad, the Overlord strategy succeeded along most of the beachhead. On four of the beaches, Allied troops were well established by noon. The hardest fighting of all, however, raged throughout the day on the fifth one, Omaha Beach. Omaha was a relatively narrow strand of shoreline, overshadowed by hundred-foot cliffs. Troops trying to land there found themselves in a horrifying position, vulnerable to machine-gun and mortar fire from gun posts above. The only route out lay through four ravines, or "exits," carved by the wind and water through the cliffs. The Germans knew all about them, of course. Because it was the broadest beach in the middle of the invasion area, and had exits inland leading to high ground, Omaha was a necessity to span the gap between the British at Gold Beach and the Americans at Utah. But it was also well defended. Neither the bombardments nor the paratroopers working behind the lines had done much to soften the gun batteries on the bluffs. The Americans who landed at Omaha were sitting ducks for the best-equipped and most experienced German battalions in the Normandy sector. General Sir Bernard L. Montgomery, who was in charge of all land-based personnel in Overlord, set down his edicts for amphibious assaults. The first one was "Speed and order of landing are the first essentials." Neither was in evidence at Omaha.

American soldiers were bewildered, their officers were confused, and their comrades were lying dead all around, in the water and on the beach. Blood was omnipresent. For hours, they didn't know what to do, and that contributed as much to the horror as did the German guns. In the chaos, there were not even any boats to evacuate the wounded, many of whom died on Omaha of injuries that would have been mere nuisances on any other beach.

The only hope for the Americans was to scale the cliffs, get to high ground behind the German defenses, and open the exits. These objectives were easier said than done amid the crushing noise, violence, and justifiable fear racing through the air over Omaha Beach. By late morning, though, some troops managed to get themselves up the cliffs in small fighting forces, taking one step after another forward. By the end of the day, at a cost too high to be measured in mere statistics, they took the beach and carved out a piece of Free France, two miles wide and six miles long.

Omaha Beach was the German Army's sternest stand at Normandy and it was there that they might have been able to drive back the Americans. Had that happened, they might have repelled the entire invasion. Field Marshal Rommel, the one man who might have managed a victory in such a close battle, was not even on the scene. By a stroke of luck for the Allies, he was at home in Germany on D-Day, celebrating his wife's birthday. As news of the invasion unfolded, he tried to redirect his defenses by telephone, at one train station or another on his way back to Normandy. He, like millions of others in Europe, was ultimately at the mercy of Adolf Hitler. On D-Day, Hitler countermanded orders to hurl the panzer reserves at Normandy. By the time he changed his mind and allowed the full brunt of Germany's defense to rush toward the invasion, the Allies had their beachhead and a growing tank corps of their own.

Operation Overlord was not over on D-Day. The invasion had only begun, but thanks to the men who made the treacherous landing and refused to turn back, it would continue. With astonishing speed, the stage managers of the operation moved tons of matériel onto the Allied beachhead, building floating docks to receive thousands of tons more. Even Omaha Beach, the scene of the most bitter fighting on June 6, was a vast and busy port by June 9. It was as though it had been there for years.

On June 10, General Montgomery invited Winston Churchill to come over to Normandy for a look. Remarkably, the prime minister agreed, traveling with several other government officials to what had so recently been Nazi territory. "Montgomery, smiling and confident," Churchill wrote, "met me at the beach as we scrambled out of our landing craft. His army had already penetrated seven or eight miles inland. There was very little firing or activity. The weather was brilliant. We drove through our limited but fertile domain in Normandy. It was pleasant to see the prosperity of the countryside. The fields were full of lovely red and white cows basking or parading in the sunshine." Only four days after the horrific morning of the 6th, a part of France was free again.

The fighting in Normandy continued after D-Day, but the Nazis were doomed. Rommel knew it. On June 17, less than two weeks after the invasion began, he returned to Germany. Once Hitler's favorite general, Rommel felt that he could be candid and direct when so many lives were at stake. He tried to persuade Hitler that the end of the war was inevitable and that the only justifiable course, for the sake of Germany, was to sue the Allies for peace. Hitler would hear none of it. On the contrary, he came to regard Rommel as a traitor. In October, faced with court-martial and almost certain execution, Rommel committed suicide.

Rommel, however, had been perfectly right. D-Day had made an Allied victory practically inevitable. To be more precise, the *men* of the invading force had made an Allied victory inevitable. These are their voices, recalling the day they—and the world—could never forget. "The only unforgivable sin in war," Eisenhower had written his brother from Great Britain, "is not doing your duty." All of the men profiled in this book did *more* than their duty. Despite seasickness, enemy fire, and near-fatal injuries, they *won*.

When historian Stephen E. Ambrose was searching for an ending to his epic narrative *D-Day*, he honed in on an interview CBS anchorman Walter Cronkite conducted in 1964. Twenty years after D-Day, Cronkite, with General Eisenhower at his side, wandered the beaches of Normandy, discussing the human cost of defeating the Nazis. "But it's a wonderful thing to remember what those fellows twenty years ago were fighting for and sacrificing for, what they did to preserve our way of life," Eisenhower said. "Not to conquer any territory, not for any ambitions of our own. But to make sure that Hitler could not destroy freedom in the world. I think it's just overwhelming. To think of the lives that were given for that principle, paying a terrible price on this beach alone, on that one day, 2,000 casualties. But they did it so that the world could be free. It just shows what free men will do rather than be slaves."

This book—published for the sixtieth anniversary of D-Day—is comprised of the reminiscences of D-Day veterans who refused to be slaves.

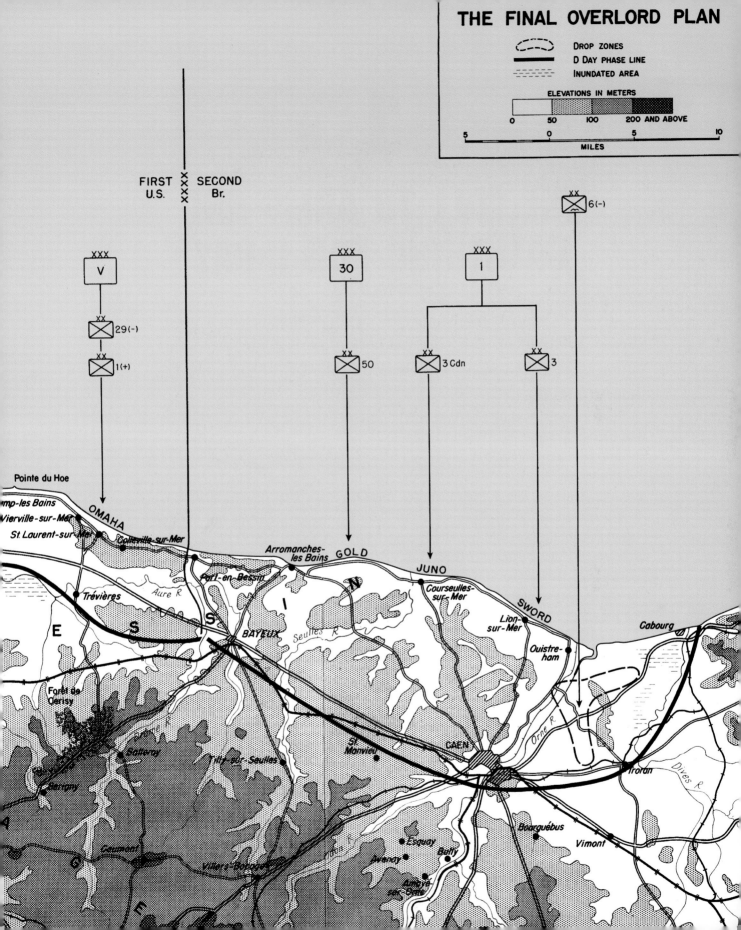

DROP ZONES
D DAY PHASE LINE
INUNDATED AREA

ELEVATIONS IN METERS

0   50   100   200 AND ABOVE

5   0   5   10

MILES

FIRST
U.S.
XXXX
SECOND
Br.

XX
6 (-)

XXX
V

XXX
30

XXX
1

XX
29 (-)

XX
1 (+)

XX
50

XX
3 Cdn

XX
3

Pointe du Hoe

mp-les Bains

Vierville-sur-Mer

St. Laurent-sur-Mer

OMAHA

Colleville-sur-Mer

Arromanches-
les Bains

GOLD

JUNO

Courseulles-
sur-Mer

SWORD

Cabourg

Trévières

Port-en-Bessin

Aure R.

Seulles R.

BAYEUX

Lion-
sur-Mer

Ouistre-
ham

Orne R.

Dives R.

Forêt de
Cerisy

Balleroy

Tilly-sur-Seulles

St.
Manvieu

CAEN

Troarn

Vimont

Cerigny

Caumont

Villers-Bocage

Esquay

Buffy

Avenay

Amayé-
sur-Orne

Bourguébus

Chapter

1

THE CALL TO ARMS AND GATHERING FOR D-DAY

On Saturday, December 6, 1941, Americans basked in the warm glow of safety ensured by the vastness of two oceans protecting their nation's flanks and by an American president who had vowed to keep them out of war.

Americans listened to the events unfolding in war-ravaged Europe, and they fought the war verbally in barbershops, corner bars, and grocery stores. But this idle chat did not translate into sentiment for another bailout of Europe as in World War I.

Most Americans were interested in the "pursuit of happiness" promised by the framers of the Constitution, and in their lifetimes, there had been little time for that. Two generations had experienced World War I or the Great Depression, or both, and the Roper and Gallup polls of the time told Franklin Roosevelt he was on solid ground to oppose American involvement. Eighty percent of Americans were opposed to war, period.

Not even the German sinking of the American ship *Reuben James* in October 1941 and the loss of close to one hundred fellow Americans could budge the population toward war. The president was forced to assure the nation that this sinking would not cause a German-American diplomatic break even as he wore a black armband in honor of the American dead.

But on December 7, everything changed. America was attacked, the youth of America heeded the call to arms, and lines formed around the blocks at recruiting stations. Americans

 Disk 1, Tracks 2–6: Enlistment and training

OPPOSITE: The lines outside recruiting offices grew dramatically following Japan's attack on Pearl Harbor in 1941.

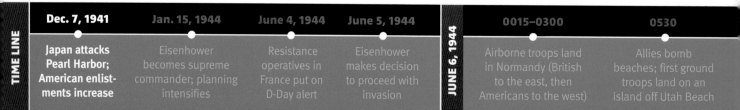

TIME LINE

Dec. 7, 1941	Jan. 15, 1944	June 4, 1944	June 5, 1944	JUNE 6, 1944	0015–0300	0530
Japan attacks Pearl Harbor; American enlistments increase	Eisenhower becomes supreme commander; planning intensifies	Resistance operatives in France put on D-Day alert	Eisenhower makes decision to proceed with invasion		Airborne troops land in Normandy (British to the east, then Americans to the west)	Allies bomb beaches; first ground troops land on an island off Utah Beach

0630	0700	0730–0745	0930–1330	1203	1300	1600	2400
H-Hour on Utah and Omaha Beaches	U.S. Army Rangers scale Pointe du Hoc	H-Hour on Gold, Sword, and Juno Beaches	Troops advance inland	British commandos meet airborne troops at Orne bridges	U.S. 4th Infantry meets 101st Airborne at Pouppeville	Tanks move inland from Omaha Beach	Five beach-heads secured; liberation under way

The staff of a U.S. Army recruiting station in Boston, Massachusetts, gather around a radio as President Franklin D. Roosevelt asks Congress for a declaration of war against Japan.

came to arms to defeat the Japanese enemy that had brought about the "Day of Infamy" at Pearl Harbor, and four days later when Germany declared war against the United States, those same Americans were happy to include the Nazis as enemies.

They came into uniform as volunteers and draftees, and they came from every state and territory, and for every possible reason. Some were too young but lied about their age or forged parents' signatures. Men came by the hundreds of thousands to fight in every corner of the world. Some came to be with their buddies, or because their older brothers were in the war, or because someone close to them had been killed.

DOUGLAS BRINKLEY AND RONALD J. DREZ

While most trips to the induction center were uneventful, with lines of men filling out forms, getting shots, and reading eye charts, they were not always routine.

F. L. Mutter had a kidney ailment that threatened to keep him out of the Army. His friends were in, and the thought of being left behind was a bitter pill.

"My patriotism was really inflated," he said. "I had decided to enlist in the Army. At the induction center, they kept me there two days, urinating in a bottle, before they gave me a rejection slip and told me I had a kidney problem. I was pretty disappointed.

"There were three of us guys who palled around together: Dinky, Arnie, and myself. Dinky got drafted, so Arnie and I went to the draft board and asked if we could all go together. Since Arnie and I were due to be drafted in a few months anyway, they approved."

But the Army's approval of that arrangement was without the knowledge that Mutter had a health problem, and he wasn't telling them. He counted on his friend Dinky to help him.

"In the induction center, we were taking our physicals, I told Dinky to save a little for my bottle, or I wouldn't pass. He did and I passed."

The paratroopers challenged Arthur Thompson. Tommy, as his friends called him, had enlisted to go into the Air Corps as a tractor driver. One day a paratrooper recruiter came to talk to his outfit. The man didn't have to say a word to get Tommy to sign up.

"Well, he had a satin jumpsuit on," said Thompson, "and boots and that little hat with that little white thing on it, and the white parachute, and he unrolled this poster, and the picture of a paratrooper and the words, 'Swoop Down on the Enemy Like a Falcon from Above. Don't Walk into the Fight, Jump.' I followed him right over there and signed up. Right there! Honest to God!"

Howard Melvin's experience joining the service was a cause for embarrassment. He had gone down to the enlistment office after being called in the draft and stood in a line of twelve men. He noticed a rather skinny fellow standing in front of him and

wondered how such a puny-looking individual could get into the Army. Melvin was short and feisty and in great shape, and had the look of a boxer.

"When we got to the end of the line," said Melvin, "they said to me, 'You didn't make it. You're not in the Army.' And the guy in front of me, the puny little guy, made it."

Melvin was humiliated and tried to explain what might have happened, but the enlistment people had no time for that. Melvin surmised that the papers had gotten switched, and that his papers had gone to the frail fellow in front of him. But it didn't change his status.

So he went down the next day to enlist and told the recruiters that he wanted to join the paratroopers. "They told me," said Melvin, "'Well, sit down in that hall there and the doctor will take care of you, because you've got to get a special examination.'

"So I waited there for about two hours, and finally I got up enough nerve to ask the sergeant, 'Hey, when is the doctor gonna come out?' 'Oh, knock on the door,' said the sergeant, so I knocked on the door, and here's a guy with a cigar in his mouth, his feet on the desk, and he says, 'What do you want?' And I said, 'Well, I'm supposed to get a special examination to join the paratroopers.'

"He said, 'Oh, that's fine. Jump up on the desk.' I jumped on the desk, and he said, 'Jump off the desk.' I jumped off the desk, and he said, 'OK, you're ready!'"

Enlistment wasn't happening only in America. Although all able-bodied men were called up in Great Britain, some not serving were anxiously trying to get into the fray. Peter Masters's enlistment was perhaps the strangest of all, because it carried with it the classification of "enemy alien."

"When the Nazis came to Austria on the 12th of March, 1938, things became so bad that my family, being Jewish, tried to get out. It took us until the 21st of August, so I lived under the Nazis for six months, which was quite sufficient to turn me from a kid that had been brought up as a pacifist to a carte blanche volunteer wanting to get part of the action against the Nazis."

DOUGLAS BRINKLEY AND RONALD J. DREZ

But when part of Masters's family managed to escape to Great Britain [some would perish at Auschwitz], they were greeted with little enthusiasm.

"I was interned by the British as an enemy alien," said Masters, "having first been classified as a 'friendly' enemy alien." But that did not last long.

Masters and many of his friends could speak German and had other skills that were attractive. Soon he found himself at an interview. "I got an interview by a visiting officer who was wearing no rank insignia, a raincoat, and dark glasses, and it turned out to be the skipper of a commando troop that was being formed from people just like me: refugees from Germany, Austria, Hungary, and some from Czechoslovakia." Masters would serve in the British Commandos.

A future 101st Airborne trooper also came from Germany, barely escaping Nazi tyranny. He was Fred Patheiger.

"I lived in Germany with my mother, grandmother, and aunt. When Hitler got into power, my mother, grandmother, and aunt had to join the party. I had to join the Hitler Youth or I couldn't have gone to school. I discovered one day, while a youngster crawling into the living room and listening to them speak, that, much to my amazement, my grandfather on my mother's side was Jewish.

"My aunt went with a fellow. They were going to get married and she owned up to him about her background, and when he found out that her father had been Jewish, well, that was it. He reported it and we were all in trouble. We had to get out of the party; I had to get out of the Hitler Youth."

Thanks to another aunt in Chicago, Patheiger and some of his family managed to escape before Nazi tyranny consumed them, but most of his family perished in Germany. He eventually enlisted in the U.S. Army and became a paratrooper.

The Army's numbers swelled during the years from 1942 until the beginning of 1944. Many of those recently enlisted Americans fought in initial battles against the Germans in North Africa and in Italy in 1943, but a tremendous number were sent to England to train as part of the enormous force required to

Fred C. Patheiger, born in Rastatt, Germany, joined the U.S. Army after fleeing to Chicago with his family. He eventually volunteered with the 101st Airborne Division.

Life went on for the British citizenry, despite being surrounded by vehicles and men on their way to France.

engage the Germans in Europe. England found its population swelled by young Americans gathering there for the cross-channel attack. The common quip was that the only things preventing the whole island from sinking into the sea from the increased weight were the barrage balloons (the tethered balloons hung above strategic locations to prevent low-flying aircraft from making strafing attacks).

Young Americans were quartered in British homes, and brought with them strange modifications to the English language. Suddenly the buzzword on London streets was "Got

DOUGLAS BRINKLEY AND RONALD J. DREZ

some gum, chum?" These young Americans were big and brash, and they had not been drained by the strains of war that had affected the population of England during the two years alone against the German might.

The evidence of the years when Britain had been alone was not lost on the arriving Americans. It was a sobering sight to see Big Ben and the Houses of Parliament surrounded by barbed wire and piles of rubble that had once been buildings.

Dan Morse, who arrived to serve in the Army Air Corps, said, "One of my most vivid memories was going through London on that speedy little English train in the middle of the blackout. It was a bright moonlit night, and the moon was shining off the silver barrage balloons that were flying above all of the railroad tracks and all of London. It was a picture that one could never forget."

Robert Wilkins from Atchison, Kansas, was surprised to be quartered in an English home. He was with the Combat Engineers, and upon arrival in England his unit was taken to the town of Paignton. He and the other soldiers rode in a truck down the streets of the small town.

"The authorities would go down the street," he said, "and the truck would stop and they would say, 'All right, three of you out here.'

"They'd march you into a house and say to the owner, 'These are your American troops. They are going to be staying with you.'

"The home I went into," said Wilkins, "the people were named Glover. Mrs. Glover made us remove our boots outside before she would even let us come in the house. We immediately thought that this was going to be a very difficult situation, and we certainly weren't happy with it at all; but after we became acquainted with the Glovers, they treated us like we were their own sons.

"Everything was blackout and we didn't do much at night. Mr. Glover would give us a piano concert in the evening, and it was a moving experience."

It was only natural to form relationships with the British people because of the close-quartered living, but it also created

PFC Harold Baumgarten, from New York City, joined the 116th Regiment, 29th Division in England. He is pictured here in Torquay, England, on March 2, 1944—his nineteenth birthday.

strained feelings. These American GIs dated British girls, which aggravated British boys, and the American soldiers were paid a little more money than the British soldiers. They were confident and, at most times, noisy.

This led to a popular refrain heard throughout England: "The problem with the Americans is that they are overpaid, oversexed, and over here!"

The American GIs were not to be intimidated by a simple ditty, and they countered with a slogan of their own: "The problem with the British lads," they would say, "is that they are underpaid, undersexed, and under Eisenhower!"

These innocent barbs eventually gave way to the greater task at hand, and that was to launch a successful cross-channel attack—a feat accomplished only twice in two thousand years. It was a daunting task, and the future of Europe, if not all of western civilization, hung in the balance.

Although the invasion area was known by only the highest ranking personnel in the combined Anglo-American brain trust, the invasion force trained in Britain for whatever mission it might be assigned.

The American division that had been in England the longest by D-Day was the 29th Division, "the Blue and Gray Division," made up of National Guard forces from Virginia and Maryland. When Harold Baumgarten from New York City arrived in Scotland in early 1944, he joined the 116th Regiment of the 29th Division, stationed in Plymouth.

"We got an introductory explanation of what we were there for and what was going to happen to us," said Baumgarten. "Colonel Canham of the 116th Infantry of the 29th Division spoke to us at Crown Barracks in Plymouth, England, and explained to us that we are going to be the first forces into the second front in Europe; and that two out of three of us aren't expected to come back, and if anybody's got butterflies in the belly, to ask for a transfer now, because it's going to be that kind of an operation."

PFC John Robertson, also of the 29th Division, described his briefing. "We were told that we were bringing the 2nd Battalion

DOUGLAS BRINKLEY AND RONALD J. DREZ

of the 116th Infantry Regiment to full strength and we would start amphibious training for the invasion because our unit had been chosen for the first wave on D-Day.

"Our camp was an English barracks and our training area was one that we were told had been used by the British Commandos. The rifle range was on the moors and was very hazardous as fierce winds whipped up without warning, blowing targets out of their holders. We dug holes on the slopes of the moors and had Sherman tanks run over us. A very frightening experience considering how mushy and wavy the moors were. It was sort of a land of trembling earth."

PFC Harry Parley of the 29th Division was a flamethrower man. "The moment of my arrival is still quite vivid. We were ushered into a room in one of the Quonset huts and told to sit on the floor. A few moments later, our new CO walked in, said his name was Captain Lawrence Madill, and that our company was to be first wave in the invasion of France, that 30 percent casualties were expected, and that we were them. As simple as that!"

Parley did not let that grim announcement spoil his sense of humor. As a flamethrower man, he was also a practical joker and relished terrorizing his buddies who did not know how his formidable weapon operated.

"While waiting to be loaded onto the ships at dockside, I would often light a cigarette using the flamethrower. Being experienced with my weapon, I knew all the safety factors. I could, without triggering the propelling mechanism, light a cigarette by simply producing a small flame at the mouth of the gun. In doing so, it produced the same hissing sound as when the thrower was actually being fired. When my team would hear the terrifying sound, I would immediately be the only one on the dock."

Part of the invasion force's training was to go out into the English Channel and make practice landings on beaches that might be similar to the actual invasion beaches—but where? The job of finding suitable training beaches had fallen to Lieutenant Colonel Paul Thompson of the 6th Engineering Special Brigade.

John Robertson served in the 116th Regiment, 29th Division on D-Day. He is shown here in a portrait from 1945 with the decorations he earned during the war, including a Presidential Unit Citation for the 116th on D-Day, and a Purple Heart.

On the beaches of Great Britain, the Allied forces trained for amphibious landings. Here an LCT unloads its cargo of tanks and men at Woolacombe, England.

"There did exist one site," he said, "with tides so wide-ranging, and surfs so rough, and weather so unpredictable that neither of the great navies nor the dashing [Lord Louis] Mountbatten had ever done more than take a look at it and run. This fearsome sight was called Woolacombe-Appledoor, or Woolacombe for short.

"At this time, I didn't appreciate another characteristic of the Woolacombe training area. . . . And that was its startling similarity to a certain coastal area in Normandy which would make the history books under a code name 'Omaha.' By March of 1944, all nine combat teams of the three D-Day

DOUGLAS BRINKLEY AND RONALD J. DREZ

assault divisions—1st, 29th, and 4th—had gone through the Woolacombe mill."

D-Day was approaching and it was time for the big American rehearsals for the invasion. These were staged on the beaches of Slapton Sands in Devonshire. The waters there were not nearly as furious as those at Woolacombe, and those final exercises would prove the readiness of the landing force that had been honed to a razor's edge.

One exercise, called Operation Tiger, took place on April 27–28, 1944. Lieutenant Eugene Bernstein, who commanded an LCT(R) [Landing Craft Tank (Rocket)], thought the exercise was very realistic. His craft was equipped with racks capable of firing 1,060 rockets as an area-saturation weapon.

"At midnight we would open a set of orders to find that we were to go to Slapton Sands. We would turn 180 degrees, make for Slapton Sands, fire our rockets on designated targets, unload attack transports into small boats, and assault the beach. These were full-scale operations with aircraft cover, major ship bombardment, the works."

But on that final training exercise something went terribly wrong. German E-boats, using utmost stealth in the dark, slipped past a destroyer screen and ran undaunted through the fleet. The speeding boats then launched a torpedo attack at the transports loaded with troops waiting to disembark for the exercise. It was a disaster.

Ewell Lunsford with the 4th Medical Battalion was on board one of the ships when the torpedoes hit.

"We lost five of the nine ships and the whole end was knocked off the one that I was on, and I was down in the hold with the vehicles and gasoline and ammunition, and just packed in there.

"I heard one torpedo come sliding down the side of the hull of the ship, and it didn't explode, and then the next one caught the stern end of it and tore off about thirty feet all the way across the end, and it was just like walking out of a big door back there. But we stayed on top. We didn't sink."

Lunsford scrambled topside as one of the E-boats made a second pass.

PFC Harry Parley trained as a flamethrower man for the 116th Regiment, 29th Division.

LST-289 was hit in the stern by a German E-boat torpedo on April 28, 1944. The enemy vessel had slipped past a screen of destroyers and wreaked havoc on transport vessels conducting a training maneuver.

"I managed to get up on top. Tracer bullets were just as thick as hair on a dog's back. I saw one of those little old E-boats in this moonlit night. I could see it coming down alongside of the ship. The guys were firing on it, and there was one ship that was along the port side that I saw him hit and it just broke in two and went down in three minutes. Everything in it went down with it."

There were over one thousand casualties with 750 men killed in the surprise attack on the fleet. Supreme headquarters immediately shrouded the event in secrecy for security purposes lest the German Army gain information. Survivors were whisked off to isolated areas and separated from their units as D-Day approached.

DOUGLAS BRINKLEY AND RONALD J. DREZ

"There never was anything in the paper about that," said Lunsford. "[No one ever] knew except one little piece in a paper from somewhere in Kentucky. Nothing was ever said about it, but when they took us ashore, they marched us way back out in those woods, away from everything. Wouldn't let us talk to anybody."

Training continued for the Allied forces in every nook and corner of southern England. All personnel trained without knowing the objective. That would be revealed only at the last minute, when the force had moved into the marshaling areas and was quarantined.

Staff Sergeant Jim Wallwork, assigned to the Glider Pilot Regiment, wondered why he and sixteen other glider pilots had been posted to the airdrome at Tarrent Rushton where there were two squadrons flying Halifax gliders and another squadron flying Horsa gliders.

Wallwork was there to perfect his flying techniques, especially night flying with a powerless glider to land in a tiny, confined field. The D-Day operation for which he trained was appropriately named Operation Deadstick.

"We began flying into a little place that was a hell of a place to choose—a small L-shaped wood about four hundred yards down the long side of the 'L' and a couple of hundred yards down the short side. That wasn't so bad in broad daylight, and we became fairly proficient until they decided to do this with night goggles [used to simulate night vision].

"You could always whip the night goggles off if you were going to overshoot, but we began to play it fairly square, realizing that whoever thought of the goggles must have had a reason."

The training for Operation Deadstick was relentless. "I did forty-three flights, many of them remote release," said Staff Sergeant Oliver Boland. "The object was to release at seven thousand feet, fly a course dead-accurate flying, with the copilot saying 'turn now,' and descend at a certain speed, which we did during the day and thirteen times at night, with no lights at all."

By the end of May 1944 Eisenhower's force was ready.

Chapter

2

LAUNCHING
THE ATTACK

General Dwight David Eisenhower's appointment came suddenly. Although he had commanded three Allied invasions in North Africa, Sicily, and Italy, the command for the invasion onto the Continent of Europe was not decided upon until the last moment.

Within the Anglo-American alliance, it had always been understood that the commander for the cross-channel attack would come from the country providing the preponderance of fighting force. If the invasion had been launched in 1943, then the supreme commander would have been British, but in 1944, America was providing the great majority of the fighting forces both on land and in the air.

In November 1943, President Franklin Roosevelt and Prime Minister Winston Churchill met in Tehran with Marshal Joseph Stalin of the Soviet Union. Russia had absorbed the fierce blows of the German Army on its home soil since 1941, and Russians died by the millions at Leningrad and Stalingrad. Stalin wanted to know when the Allies would open the second front that would offer his blood-drained country some relief.

Roosevelt deferred and said a decision had not yet been made. Stalin was miffed. He expressed distrust in his allies and stated that until a commander was named, he would not believe that a second front would be opened.

Disk 1, Tracks 7–9: Final preparations for the invasion

OPPOSITE: British prime minister Winston Churchill (front, left) sits with United States president Franklin D. Roosevelt (front, right). Between the two leaders stands Admiral Lord Louis Mountbatten.

TIME LINE

Dec. 7, 1941	Jan. 15, 1944	June 4, 1944	June 5, 1944	JUNE 6, 1944	0015–0300	0530
Japan attacks Pearl Harbor; American enlistments increase	**Eisenhower becomes supreme commander; planning intensifies**	Resistance operatives in France put on D-Day alert	Eisenhower makes decision to proceed with invasion		Airborne troops land in Normandy (British to the east, then Americans to the west)	Allies bomb beaches; first ground troops land on an island off Utah Beach

0630	0700	0730–0745	0930–1330	1203	1300	1600	2400
H-Hour on Utah and Omaha Beaches	U.S. Army Rangers scale Pointe du Hoc	H-Hour on Gold, Sword, and Juno Beaches	Troops advance inland	British commandos meet airborne troops at Orne bridges	U.S. 4th Infantry meets 101st Airborne at Pouppeville	Tanks move inland from Omaha Beach	Five beach-heads secured; liberation under way

In early December, Roosevelt and Churchill continued to Cairo, Egypt, for more talks. As the last meeting was breaking up on December 6, Roosevelt had General Marshall scribble a note to send to Stalin stating, "The immediate appointment of General Eisenhower to command of Overlord operation has been decided upon." Roosevelt signed the note immediately and also announced his decision to Churchill. On January 15, 1944, Eisenhower became Supreme Commander, Allied Expeditionary Force.

Eisenhower inherited the Overlord plan sketched out in 1943 by Lieutenant General Frederick Morgan who served at the post of Chief of Staff to the Supreme Allied Command (COSSAC). Morgan had drawn the plan based on a number of factors that limited his scope. The shortage of landing craft for an invasion did not allow for multiple landings along the French coast and limited the assault to three divisions attacking on a narrow front.

Geography limited the attack, as well. It had to be within the range of fighter aircraft flying from England, and had to take place across beaches that had the ability to support unloading operations until a port could be captured and opened. It also had to be at a location that would facilitate follow-up maneuvering that would target the heartland of Germany. The obvious choice was Pas-de-Calais, just twenty-five miles across the channel from Dover, and the shortest route to Berlin.

But the Germans also recognized that Calais was the ideal landing spot, so they made the fortifications virtually impregnable. The low shelving beaches between the Caen Canal and the Cotentin Peninsula on the Normandy coast offered COSSAC an area meeting the stringent requirements. Aerial photographs also showed that the constructed defenses were relatively light.

When Eisenhower took command, he modified the plan to increase the three-division landing force to five, and added airborne divisions to secure the flanks of the battle area. He also extended the invasion front to the west to land on the Cotentin Peninsula, thereby placing infantry closer to the large port of Cherbourg.

DOUGLAS BRINKLEY AND RONALD J. DREZ

General Dwight D. Eisenhower (shown at left) took command of the vast Allied operation on January 15, 1944. Here he oversees training with British Field Marshal Sir Bernard Law Montgomery (far right).

But for Eisenhower to have a chance at success, he had to deceive the Germans as to where the attack would come, so they could not unleash their overwhelmingly superior force against him at his point of attack. The vulnerability of an amphibious invasion is that the invading force starts with nothing ashore and builds up from the first man who lands on the beach. Arrayed against that first soldier is the full strength of the defending forces if they know where the attack will take place. To attempt to confuse the enemy, Eisenhower adopted the British deception plan called Operation Fortitude.

As the war progressed, so did the battle to safeguard the secret: a war of plots and counterplots, tangles within tangles, double agents, false agents, treachery, cloaks and daggers, and gold. Deceptions and lies were melded with tantalizing bits of truth, emerging in tales to throw the Germans off the track.

The Allies were not the only ones to initiate spy operations. In Germany, Hitler had ordered the Abwehr to deluge the United Kingdom with spies. Some were flown to England and dropped by parachute at night into the countryside to

melt into the mainstream of the British population. Others came by sea.

Pretty soon, radios at the Abwehr's headquarters in Hamburg crackled with news from their agents. Secret messages sent from inside England described troop concentrations, hidden airfields, gun emplacements, antiaircraft locations, and other critical data. The message traffic was steady. Some casualties occurred and some radios suddenly went silent, but all in all, the Germans considered their spy operation a success.

However, the German perception of its spy operation was in itself a deception. In reality, the Abwehr's operation was a disaster, and as each day went by, it became more disastrous. The fact was that every single spy ever dispatched to England had been arrested—a remarkable feat in itself. The captured spies were made the proverbial offer they could not refuse: turn or hang. Become a double agent or face the hangman's noose. Most chose the former and pretended to work for the Fatherland when, in fact, they were working for their captors. The information they sent from Britain was only what the Allies wanted released. Without knowing it, the Abwehr had fallen victim to a gigantic deception operation called Operation Double Cross.

While Operation Fortitude seduced German intelligence, the Overlord planners faced their own operational problems. Once the Normandy invasion area had been selected, there remained only the question of when. The factors contributing to the selection of the date were many.

Dawn would be the time, chosen because the great armada needed the cover of darkness to arrive in the attack area with the least possibility of detection. The early time of attack would also give the Allied forces a full day of light to attempt to establish a beachhead and consolidate their positions.

The phase of the moon and the level of the tides were vital. It was imperative that the great landing force come ashore with a low tide to expose underwater obstacles that could rip the bottoms out of landing craft or explode attached mines. But landing at low tide would require that the soldiers make a long wade

DOUGLAS BRINKLEY AND RONALD J. DREZ

in before they could reach the beach and work their way to the draws. Meanwhile, the bombers and paratroopers needed at least a half-moon to conduct successful air operations.

Finally, the invasion had to come late enough in the year to allow final springtime training in England, but also early enough so that the invading forces would have at least four months of good campaigning weather before the onset of winter. This list of imposing criteria could be met only three times in all of 1944: the first few days in May and the second and third weeks in June.

"We had to have a particular combination of tides, light, and moon," said General Eisenhower. "You had a couple of days in May, and a couple of days in June. We would like to have gone on the 5th of May."

But the May 5 goal proved to be wishful thinking and was short-lived. The Allied planners counted up the landing craft needed for the attack and found that they were 271 short. Eisenhower chose to move the date back to June 5 in order to allow a month for industrial production to close the gap.

Churchill was frustrated and growled that the destinies of the "two greatest empires seemed to be tied up in some goddam thing called LSTs."

But LSTs (Landing Ship, Tank) were not the only problem facing the Allies. An internal conflict threatened to sunder the carefully forged alliance.

As the date of the invasion came closer, Eisenhower was faced with a dilemma. It was imperative for him to isolate the battlefield, and that meant diverting the bombing of other targets. Eisenhower argued that while attacking German oil sources and infrastructure would have the long-term effect of destruction of an important enemy resource and would be decisive, the immediate success of the cross-channel attack rested in the ability to keep the enemy from reinforcing the battlefield. To accomplish this, he favored the Transportation Plan, which targeted rolling stock, marshaling yards, bridges, and other targets that would hinder the German Army's ability to move to the landing area during those first critical days

FOR EISENHOWER TO HAVE A CHANCE AT SUCCESS, HE HAD TO DECEIVE THE GERMANS AS TO WHERE THE ATTACK WOULD COME, SO THEY COULD NOT UNLEASH THEIR OVERWHELMINGLY SUPERIOR FORCE AGAINST HIM AT HIS POINT OF ATTACK.

PFC William (Bill) Tucker, 505th Parachute Infantry Regiment, 82nd Airborne Division. This picture was taken in August 1944, after Tucker's return from Normandy.

of lodgment and buildup when an amphibious attack was most vulnerable.

The resistance to Eisenhower's plan was such that he felt his authority as supreme commander was being undermined. After enduring much bickering, he resolved the impasse by announcing that if he were not allowed to use the air forces that had been entrusted to him as he saw fit to accomplish the mission, he would resign and go home. Needless to say, he prevailed, but his willingness to resign from the most prestigious military command in the history of modern warfare spoke volumes of Eisenhower's dedication to his plan, to his men, and to Allied victory.

As the months before D-Day dwindled to weeks, the deception plan moved into high gear. From the beginning, the German High Command contended that George Patton was America's best general and would be at the spear point of the Allied attack. Eisenhower was delighted to take advantage of this misconception.

First United States Army Group (FUSAG), commanded by General Patton, was positioned around Dover where it appeared poised to attack Pas-de-Calais. Many of Patton's tanks and trucks were rubber models easily lifted by two men but capable of deceiving aerial photographs. Patton himself appeared often in public to fix his location in the German mind. FUSAG was a shell of an army.

More remarkable was the British 4th Army. While FUSAG was not the force it appeared to be, the 4th Army didn't exist at all. Several dozen middle-age to over-age British officers, with an accompanying entourage of radio operators, settled in the far reaches of Scotland in a room beneath Edinburgh Castle. Through radio traffic, this tiny force tried to create, in the German mind, a prodigious, 250,000-man army capable of invading Norway.

They must have had some success, because Hitler reinforced Norway's garrison, bringing it up to thirteen divisions. The German High Command was led to believe that Eisenhower had eighty-nine divisions when, in fact, he only had forty-seven.

DOUGLAS BRINKLEY AND RONALD J. DREZ

First United States Army Group (FUSAG) was perhaps the greatest fake army ever assembled. The decoy tanks (such as the one shown here) and other vehicles were positioned near Dover, England, where they appeared ready for transport to Pas-de-Calais—the section of France the Allies wanted Hitler to think they would strike.

Toward the end of May, the great force moved into the marshaling areas where they were quarantined: no one in, no one out. Men with dental emergencies were taken out under guard and then returned to the quarantined areas.

In the area of the 505th Parachute Infantry Regiment (PIR) of the 82nd Airborne Division, speculation ran wild. PFC Bill Tucker, from Massachusetts, read to pass the time.

"I started to read a book, and it got quite interesting, *A Tree Grows in Brooklyn*. At the sand tables, we were all making bets. There were guys saying we are going to jump in Norway, Yugoslavia, etcetera. When they took off the cover at the sand table, they had a complete layout and aerial photograph of Sainte-Mère-Église.

"Well my reaction wasn't anything startling. I was old enough to realize that we weren't going to jump into the Ruhr. France was the place. The word 'Normandy' was to me a romantic word. It

Ed Jeziorski was a machine gunner for the 507th Parachute Infantry Regiment. Though it is difficult to see in this picture (taken shortly after the Normandy campaign), Jeziorski recalls that small pieces of each of his ears were already missing then—evidence of near-misses by the enemy.

was not just France, it was Normandy, and I read enough to be intrigued. It was the biggest thing in history at the time."

"One of the advantages we had when we went into Normandy was that the landscape hadn't changed in a hundred years, and all the maps were exceedingly accurate," said Sergeant Howard Melvin. It would be the third combat jump for the 505th, and Melvin knew that some things would go wrong. But they were ready.

"The jumps into Sicily and Italy were also at night. We had the experience and we felt that we could handle the situation. . . . We knew that it was not going to go by the numbers as they exactly planned it. The airplanes in Sicily and Italy had broken formations."

Joseph Blaylock from Wiggins, Mississippi, was assigned to the 20th Field Artillery of the 4th Division. "Around the first part of June we got ready to pull out of Crompton down into the marshaling areas, and the whole town turned out to say goodbye to us, because they had a feeling and we had a feeling that this was the real thing.

"On June 3, we were called into a big tent and were given a talk by General Barton [Commanding General 4th Division], and then some of the commanders had taken over and broke us into groups, as far as telling us where we were going to make Utah Beach, and also explained to us where Omaha Beach would be, and then where the French and the English and the Canadians would be, and they told us about Normandy. So, they gave us even the pear tree, or apple tree, that we would be under as far as putting our gun positions. That's how precise it was."

The men also had clothing impregnated with chemicals to provide protection should the Germans introduce gas warfare. "During this time," said Edward Jeziorski, a machine gunner with the 507th PIR, "we had all been ordered to turn in one jumpsuit to be impregnated with some kind of stuff." A week or so later, he got back his newly impregnated jumpsuit.

"We received our jumpsuits and put those suckers on. I want to tell all they were the lousiest, the coldest, the clammiest, the stiffest, the stinkiest articles of clothing that were ever dreamed up to be worn by individuals. Surely the guy that was responsible for the idea on this screwup received a Distinguished Service Medal from the devil himself."

The U.S. 1st Infantry Division, known as "the Big Red One," was assembled in an area north of London.

"Captain Briggs, our company commander, assembled the entire company, ordered trucks, and drove to a large field," said Joseph Dragotto. "In the field were assembled many thousands [of] American troops, and over a loudspeaker, I heard the word 'Attention.'

"In the corner of my eye, I could see two men—one wearing an American uniform, the other a British uniform. As they came closer, I recognized them. The American was General Eisenhower, the supreme Allied commander, and the other was Field Marshal Montgomery. Both men stepped onto the platform and spoke to the men. General Eisenhower said we were about to embark on a great cause: 'the liberation of Europe, and God be with you.' Montgomery said almost the same thing, but added that he was grateful for the help and the troops, talking to them. And then General Eisenhower stopped in front of me. I thought to myself, My God, the supreme commander of all the Allied forces in Europe is going to talk to me! The general asked where I was from and how long I was in the service."

On May 29, General Eisenhower moved to Southwick House near Portsmouth. The skies were clear and the Channel was calm. The launching of Operation Neptune (the Channel crossing) was at hand. In one week, the great armada would cross to Normandy for the long-anticipated attack.

But on June 1 the first disquieting reports of bad weather sifted into Supreme Headquarters, forcing Group Captain Richard Staggs, head of the Meteorological Committee, to alert Eisenhower that the forecast for June 4, 5, and 6 was not good.

June 4 would be the critical day of decision for deciding whether or not to invade on June 5. The assault troops would already be loaded in their craft and ready to go. At 0400, Staggs gave a troubling report. Even though the weather outside was

Joseph Blaylock served in the Army's 20th Field Artillery of the 4th Infantry Division.

While the Allied leadership decided whether or not to proceed with the operation in the early days of June, the troops boarded their vessels—ready to proceed unless called back.

deceivingly calm, he forecast deteriorating weather for D-Day that would yield force 5 winds and a low cloud base of five hundred feet.

"That morning," said Eisenhower, "the stars were out and beautiful and he gave us the worst report you ever saw."

Eisenhower polled his deputies. A few wanted to go, but most wanted to postpone. The key factor was air operations. The terrible weather would hinder the parachute drops and affect bombing accuracy. This led to other problems. The endangered paratroop drops would also jeopardize the landings at Utah. Without the paratroopers to control the narrow causeways leading off the beach, the Germans could mass forces to

DOUGLAS BRINKLEY AND RONALD J. DREZ

crush the 4th Division's attack across the beach. Eisenhower decided to postpone for one day. D-Day was reset for June 6.

The great armada, already at sea, was called back. The paratroopers stood down for twenty-four hours. The supreme commander and his staff would meet again at 2130 that evening for an update.

Lieutenant Dean Stockwell's LCT group was already on the water. "Finally, about daybreak," he said, "we could see what was going on and see we were under way along the coast of England and in the English Channel, headed roughly eastward toward the rendezvous point with other groups coming from the east, from Southampton and Portsmouth, and places like that. Should the weather make the landing unsafe, we were to be notified by a simple message called 'Post Mike One.'

"Early in the afternoon of June 4, a picket boat came alongside LCT 535—from which I was commanding the sixteen landing craft—and handed me a telegram that simply said, 'Post Mike One.' So, we all turned around, hundreds and hundreds of ships of various sizes, and headed back to our respective departure points."

At the British airfield at Tarrant Rushton, Major John Howard and his special glider-borne force waited for the word that the invasion was on. A code word would tell him.

"Every morning at transit camp," said Howard, "a dispatch rider on a motorbike came down from 6th Airborne Division headquarters which was at Harwell in Oxfordshire. He would give me a one-word message, a code word, and that code word meant either 'you are not going tonight,' or 'you are going tonight.' The code word that meant we were going was 'Cromwell.' On Sunday, June 4—and I was a bit surprised because the weather was getting so bad—I got 'Cromwell.' I immediately called the officers together and told them and we started preparing to go that night. We had our fatless meal, but soon after, I got another message that it was canceled. I then had to give the deflating news right down the line again, and as a result, we all had a pretty rotten night."

At Portsmouth, Group Captain Staggs rushed toward Southwick House for the 2130 meeting that would determine if

EISENHOWER POLLED HIS DEPUTIES. A FEW WANTED TO GO, BUT MOST WANTED TO POSTPONE. THE KEY FACTOR WAS AIR OPERATIONS. THE TERRIBLE WEATHER WOULD HINDER THE PARACHUTE DROPS AND AFFECT BOMBING ACCURACY.

THE GREAT ARMADA, ALREADY AT SEA, WAS CALLED BACK. THE PARATROOPERS STOOD DOWN FOR TWENTY-FOUR HOURS. THE SUPREME COMMANDER AND HIS STAFF WOULD MEET AGAIN AT 2130 THAT EVENING [JUNE 5] FOR AN UPDATE.

D-Day had to be postponed again. After having given the forecast that morning that had led Eisenhower to postpone, he had spent the rest of the day poring over weather charts. He saw the edge of the front that would pass through Portsmouth that evening, and then examined the depression that would follow on its heels.

But that front was now intensifying and strengthening, and this intensification was slowing its forward progress. Staggs was excited. A small gap seemed to be developing between the two weather systems, and that gap might translate into a small window of improved weather.

But not all members of the meteorological team agreed with Staggs. Heated arguments lasted more than two hours. A second conference later during the day still did not produce a consensus.

Staggs arrived at Southwick as gale-force winds drove the pouring rain horizontally into the windowpanes. He entered the conference room filled with tenseness. He began his straightforward report with a stoic voice. He reported that the cloud conditions should be better and the winds not so strong after midnight. The weather would be tolerable, but not more than that.

Again Eisenhower polled his lieutenants, and finally said, "I'm quite positive the order must be given . . . I don't like it, but there it is." Operation Overlord slipped back into gear. Within hours the great armada would roll out into the English Channel to assemble and sail to Normandy. Eisenhower would attempt the first successful cross-channel attack since William the Conqueror pulled it off in 1066.

Eisenhower ordered a final meeting for 0415 on June 5. It would be the last opportunity to call the armada back if Staggs was wrong. If Eisenhower called it back, it could not be launched again until June 19.

Staggs noted that he had recommended postponement of D-Day while the outside weather had been relatively calm and now he was recommending launching the attack in the midst of a raging storm. Would the German meteorologists also have seen the glitch in the weather charts? Would the Germans be ready?

DOUGLAS BRINKLEY AND RONALD J. DREZ

At 0415 the weather was worse. Staggs entered the mess room at Southwick to give his final report. He noted that Eisenhower was spruced and immaculately dressed. "Faces were grave and the room was silent," he said.

"The morning of the 5th, I came over here," said General Eisenhower. "The weather was terrible. This house was shaking."

The general gave him the signal to begin. Staggs stated the obvious: that the conditions had not changed, but if there was any change, it was for the better. He felt that the storm would break before dawn, but that break would only last through Tuesday. The weather would deteriorate again on Wednesday.

Eisenhower brightened and again polled his subordinates. Again there was a mixed review, with most wanting to go and only two officers voicing some reluctance.

Although Winston Churchill grumbled about holding up the invasion to wait for more landing craft to be produced, Eisenhower insisted on the delay. These craft would be indispensable to the Allied invasion.

General Erwin Rommel (far left) was responsible for German defenses in Normandy. It was Rommel who had obstacles and fortifications added along this stretch of the coast. He guessed correctly that Normandy could be a target, but misjudged on the timing of the attack.

"I thought it was the best of a bad bargain," said the general. After a pause of half a minute, he issued his historic command. "OK, let's go!"

Across the channel, the German meteorologist Walter Stoebe had forecast a period of disturbed weather during the time of advantageous moon and tides. Like Staggs he had seen the weather charts, but unlike Staggs, he predicted no gap between the fronts marching across the English Channel. With that forecast, General Erwin Rommel decided to proceed with his June 5 trip back to Germany to see Adolf Hitler. The German consensus was that the Allies could not launch an attack for another two weeks, when June 19 would offer favorable conditions.

DOUGLAS BRINKLEY AND RONALD J. DREZ

Near Colleville-sur-Mer on the Normandy Coast, Private Franz Gockel, with the 3rd Kompanie, 726 Infanterie Regiment, stood at his position at *Widerstandsnest* 62 (Resistance Nest 62, abbreviated WN 62). It was a twenty-man position with two new casemates for 75mm guns. It had recently been completed after General Rommel had inspected the Normandy Coast in February and found the defenses lacking. Between the draws at Colleville-sur-Mer and Vierville-sur-Mer, six miles to the west, Rommel had installed fifteen of these casemated positions—they were numbered 59 to 74.

"I was very young," said Gockel. "I had celebrated my eighteenth birthday in my position at *Widerstandsnest* 62. Almost half of my comrades were also eighteen and nineteen. We had an *Oberfeldwebel* [staff sergeant], two NCOs, and seventeen enlisted. The alert condition had been raised since the end of May. The veterans were saying, 'Something's in the air,' and it was reported that in southern England, strong troop units had been embarked. West of WN 62 toward WN 64, two machine-gun positions were added, and one hundred meters from our position a dummy gun position with a long barrel was erected. The weapons of WN 62 consisted of two Czechoslovakian 75mm field guns, a 50mm antitank gun, 50mm mortar, two light machine guns, and two heavy Polish machine guns. In addition, each man was equipped with his K98 carbine.

"During the evening hours, just like so often before, a debate raged in the bunker over the possibility of invasion. With heated argument, one group was convinced that the English or Americans would never attempt to land here. The other group could not be swayed from the opinion that within no more than four weeks, the 'Tommys and Amis' would be attempting to land on this beach. In accordance with orders, we slept in full uniform, only pulling our boots off and carefully placing them next to the bunks. I said to one of my comrades, 'I hope we don't have more of those damned exercise alerts tonight.'"

STAGGS NOTED THAT HE HAD RECOMMENDED POSTPONEMENT OF D-DAY WHILE THE OUTSIDE WEATHER HAD BEEN RELATIVELY CALM AND NOW HE WAS RECOMMENDING LAUNCHING THE ATTACK IN THE MIDST OF A RAGING STORM. WOULD THE GERMAN METEOROLOGISTS ALSO HAVE SEEN THE GLITCH IN THE WEATHER CHARTS? WOULD THE GERMANS BE READY?

THE BATTLEFIELD ISOLATED: HELP FROM THE RESISTANCE AND THE SOE

As Eisenhower gave the order to launch the invasion, other forces were already at work in an unending attempt to isolate the battlefield and prevent German reinforcements from moving into the attack area. The Allies now faced the reality of actually setting foot on the invasion beaches. Up until now it had been all plans and rehearsals, and on paper it was bold and daring. But the reality of the invasion was that it was one throw of the dice against the German might.

What distinguished the Normandy plan from most battle plans was that there was no alternate. There was no fallback position. There was no second chance to make advances elsewhere if the main attack failed. If the main attack failed, the invasion was doomed. At Normandy, Eisenhower could expect to face the forces of two combined German armies: the 7th, already at Normandy, and the more powerful 15th at Pas-de-Calais.

The German armored divisions could utilize the fields and roads of the French countryside to maneuver and swiftly counterattack the invasion area. Once the Allied attack began, the

Disk 1, Tracks 10–11: Undercover work in France

OPPOSITE: Resistance fighters and saboteurs in France aided Allied invaders by destroying or delaying rail lines, thus hindering German transport to the invasion area.

TIME LINE	Dec. 7, 1941	Jan. 15, 1944	June 4, 1944	June 5, 1944	JUNE 6, 1944	0015–0300	0530
	Japan attacks Pearl Harbor; American enlistments increase	Eisenhower becomes supreme commander; planning intensifies	**Resistance operatives in France put on D-Day alert**	Eisenhower makes decision to proceed with invasion		Airborne troops land in Normandy (British to the east, then Americans to the west)	Allies bomb beaches; first ground troops land on an island off Utah Beach

0630	0700	0730–0745	0930–1330	1203	1300	1600	2400
H-Hour on Utah and Omaha Beaches	U.S. Army Rangers scale Pointe du Hoc	H-Hour on Gold, Sword, and Juno Beaches	Troops advance inland	British commandos meet airborne troops at Orne bridges	U.S. 4th Infantry meets 101st Airborne at Pouppeville	Tanks move inland from Omaha Beach	Five beachheads secured; liberation under way

WHAT DISTINGUISHED THE
NORMANDY PLAN FROM
MOST BATTLE PLANS
WAS THAT THERE WAS NO
ALTERNATE. THERE WAS NO
FALLBACK POSITION.
THERE WAS NO SECOND
CHANCE TO MAKE ADVANCES
ELSEWHERE IF THE MAIN
ATTACK FAILED.

German High Command could call upon its reserve forces dispersed throughout the country to close on the battle area and thus present the Allied attacking armies with an overwhelmingly superior force. If the Germans could counterattack while the Allied landing force was still feeble and disorganized as it struggled to gain a foothold, they could crush it and hurl it back into the sea.

Eisenhower had conducted the bombing campaign to target rail yards and rolling stock in an effort to hinder German ability to reinforce the battlefield with these massive forces, and in attacking railway marshaling yards he had inflicted significant damage on the German ability to move by rail. Almost fifteen hundred locomotives were damaged or destroyed during the implementation of the Transportation Plan. But bombing also had its shortcomings, especially when targeting dispersed and camouflaged rail assets of the railway lines.

"Bombing railways was not a very satisfactory method of destroying them," said British agent Anthony Brooks, who worked with the French Resistance. "They were fairly easy to repair and cannoning them was pretty well useless. Hitting them with a bomb was very difficult at low altitude and usually they had lightweight ack-ack which protected them and [made them] an expensive air force target.

"Marshaling yards, which were good targets, tended to be near big towns, and therefore a lot of French would be killed by bombing operations. This didn't mean they wouldn't bomb marshaling yards, but that was a consideration."

In early 1944, the British secret agency responsible for sabotage and intelligence came under control of Eisenhower and the Supreme Command. This office—the SOE or Special Operations Executive—had been founded in July 1940 by Winston Churchill, who wanted to create a fighting spirit among the people who had been overrun by the German forces. His succinct order was to "set Europe ablaze," and he envisioned small groups of demolitionists, specially equipped and trained, creating havoc among the German forces. This harassing force was also built to cooperate with Allied armies whenever an invasion came.

DOUGLAS BRINKLEY AND RONALD J. DREZ

The destruction of railways in occupied France was a priority for the Allied leaders. Here the U.S. 9th Air Force bombs railway targets in May 1944 as part of the Transportation Plan. Although this bombing was successful, it was often more effective to neutralize targets from the ground. For this, the Allies relied on the SOE and French saboteurs.

SOE headquarters was located on Baker Street in London, and the office responsible for operations in France was called "F Section," commanded by Colonel Morris Buckmaster. He had been one of the last men evacuated from Dunkirk in 1940 as the German Army overran France.

"I was, I think, the last man out of Dunkirk because I happened to have been bilingually French and my general said to me, 'It won't matter if you get caught by the Germans because all you've got to do is to take off your tunic and your cap and become a Frenchman.'"

Because of his bilingual talent, Buckmaster was recruited into SOE and eventually made commander of the French section in September 1941.

He succeeded in eventually finding 480 agents, including forty women. He ordered them to parachute into France and to investigate and recruit suitable people from within the French Resistance for the job of sabotage. Arms, explosives, and equipment could then be parachuted in for their deadly work.

"You had to choose people to work in a part of France where they wouldn't be known from pre-war knowledge," said Buckmaster. "They had to have a cover story which gave them

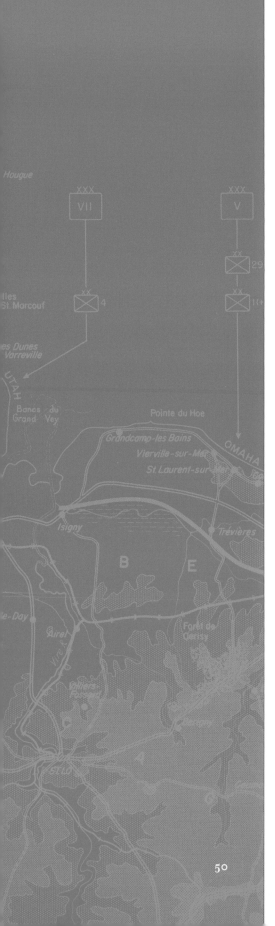

a reason for being in that area, and they had to learn their parts so well they believed them to be true themselves. If they were woken up in the middle of the night and were asked a question, they answered it in the role of the person they were representing and not in their true personality."

As D-Day approached, the SOE was added to General Eisenhower's arsenal of weapons to hinder the German capacity to maneuver and react to the upcoming invasion.

"There were two objectives to be reached," said Buckmaster. "The primary—and the important—directive was making the preparations for D-Day. We didn't know whether there ever would be a D-Day in 1943, but we assumed that the only way in which the Germans could be vanquished would be by a landing on the continent."

Sabotage on the ground was just the tool Eisenhower needed to overcome the shortcomings of aerial bombardment of railway targets. But how could orders be transmitted in a timely fashion to dispersed cells of the Resistance? The French called these underground forces the *maquis*, and although the *maquisards* were anxious for battle against the Germans, coordinating a possible attack to be launched on an undetermined D-Day was impossible.

Controlling the *maquis* was in itself difficult. They were not bands of romantic French citizens in their jaunty berets fighting for patriotism. Most *maquisards* were hard-core Communists and Socialists and members of other splinter groups filled with the zeal of hatred for the occupying Germans. They carried out their harassing attacks ruthlessly, with little regard for innocent bystanders.

"The Communist Party spent their time lobbing grenades into cinemas, cafes, *soldatenheim* [barracks], and mixed cafes," said agent Brooks, "where there might be quite genuine French people, resisters talking, and five or six Germans drinking beer and laughing. They would just lob a grenade through the glass window, possibly not even kill a German."

Even if including the *maquis* in coordinated attacks were somehow possible by orders over the radio, security would be destroyed. A sudden flood of radio traffic issuing a mountain of

The Germans realized the aerial threat to their rail cars, and mounted antiaircraft guns to them, like the one pictured here. But these guns were not effective against ground-based saboteurs.

orders to the far-flung *maquis* would be a dead giveaway to the monitoring Germans that the invasion was at hand.

The Allied planners quickly realized that targets would have to be prearranged and then triggered by a preset message to ensure overall success and not expose the Resistance.

Supreme Headquarters devised *Plan Vert* and *Plan Tortue*. The first was to attack German rail assets; SOE targeted 571 railroad sites. *Plan Tortue* called for hit-and-run guerilla tactics on bridges and highways and German columns moving toward the invasion area. Both of these plans were to begin execution upon receipt of coded orders. Every unit of the Resistance would have a specific job.

The orders to the *maquis* and other clandestine units would be delivered via the BBC (British Broadcasting Corporation).

Although this German Tiger tank appears to be loaded on a giant trailer, these dangerous tanks of the 2nd Panzer division, or *Das Reich*, were usually transported on special flat railcars, making them obvious targets for the saboteurs.

SOE prepared an enormous number of messages throughout the war for its fifty-nine radio operators and all the agents in the field. There were two messages for each unit, and the first would be the "alert" message. The second was the "action" message.

The alert message told the recipients to listen each night for the action message. The individual or group leader might hear the alert message numerous times, but until he heard the action message, he was to do nothing.

As it turned out, the Germans *had* infiltrated one of the largest SOE units and captured its alert and action messages. The messages for this infiltrated cell were from a poem, *"Chanson d'Automne,"* by the French poet Paul Verlaine. The alert message was the poem's first line: "The long sobs of the violins of autumn." The action message was the second line: "Wound my heart with a monotonous languor." The Germans knew that if they heard the second line, the invasion would occur within forty-eight hours.

But this compromised message had been scheduled for replacement and would have become useless to the Germans except for an administrative error. Instead of discarding this message, someone reassigned it to another *réseau* (Resistance cell). The Germans now had a key to tell them when the invasion would come. They only had to listen.

"The messages that we used to receive by radio were not related to the dates," said Anthony Brooks. "They were related to the full moon, and one always listened, regardless, seven days before the full moon, and that is when you got your warning messages on the BBC."

A stoic, almost disembodied voice droned the messages out by the hundreds over the air and always repeated them twice. They were nonsensical sentences, such as, "Flora has a red neck"; or "The centipede is a mammal." They were meaningless to all except the knowing individual.

The action message for Anthony Brooks, who worked as a clandestine saboteur in the Montauban area of France, was one he could never forget.

"The Montauban-area message was, '*Tetty, laisse tic re tranquil,*'" he said ("Tetty, give that bad habit a rest"). Tetty was the eldest daughter of his local boss who ran a garage, and she had long Edwardian ringlets of hair, and she was always twirling them, and twisting them, and pulling on them, and when her mother could stand the distraction no more, she'd smack the girl and order her to stop with those words. That repeated exclamation stuck in everyone's mind. Brooks thought there was no way any of his group would ever forget the mother's outbursts. So, "*Tetty, laisse tic re tranquil*" became their D-Day action message.

In April the German 2nd Panzer Division, called *Das Reich*, began to arrive in the Montauban area. Brooks and his unit noticed that the large Tiger tanks were moved into the area on special flat railcars. The massive tanks weighed over sixty tons and were real fuel guzzlers averaging only one half mile per gallon of fuel, so the Germans moved them by rail on these special cars to an attack assembly area.

These cars were enormous, with six big wheels on either end. The steel bed of the car dipped low to the tracks. Two flatcars

SABOTAGE ON THE GROUND WAS JUST THE TOOL EISENHOWER NEEDED TO OVERCOME THE SHORTCOMINGS OF AERIAL BOMBARDMENT OF RAILWAY TARGETS. BUT HOW COULD ORDERS BE TRANSMITTED IN A TIMELY FASHION TO DISPERSED CELLS OF THE RESISTANCE?

General Rommel inspects a
coastal battery in March 1944.

with Tigers loaded on could not pass each other on adjacent
tracks since the overhang was too wide.

The Germans dispersed these vital flatbeds on tracks all
around the French countryside and camouflaged them from aerial observation. But in so doing, they raised the eyebrows of
Brooks and his saboteurs.

"We realized that they were obviously very special, very
valuable, and secondly that the Germans realized this and that
is why they were dispersing them. Well of course by dispersing
them it made them that much more vulnerable to us because,
while they were in the marshaling yard, we couldn't really get
near them. So we then set about organizing girls and men and

DOUGLAS BRINKLEY AND RONALD J. DREZ

wives. We spread the briefing around through school friends, the famous Tetty and her boyfriend went often with a lot of them, and later we fitted them with a little bit of bent piping which had been hammered to fit the bolt."

The idea was to remove the bottom plug and drain out the oil in the bearing case and replace the plug. The oil had to be carried off in a small container so as not to leave any evidence of tampering. Then, upon removing the top plug of the case, the saboteur would empty a paper packet containing carborundum powder.

"The roller bearings running dry with carborundum powder was not the best form of lubrication," said Brooks. "And we did this to about 70 to 75 percent of those flats during the period up to D-Day." When a sabotaged flatcar was loaded with a Tiger tank and began rolling, it didn't take long for the wheel to seize up and for the car to derail.

"We got the warning message," said Brooks, "and then we got the 'Tetty' message on the night of the 4th of June and again on the 5th. The concept was to push the Germans onto the roads. This was for two reasons. The Germans were, on the whole, short of fuel and short on rubber tires, and their tanks and tracked vehicles had limited range. Also, the roads in France tended to be straight, out in the open country, and a convoy on a straight road was a sitting duck for cannon fire."

When Brooks got his "Tetty" message, he began to distribute the explosives that he'd accumulated for over a year. They had come via parachute drops and had been hidden at great personal risk until the day of use. If a man had a cesspool, a hundred pounds of explosives could be wrapped in sacks and lowered down into the sewerage by rope with the end held up by a little piece of wood floating on top of the malodorous muck.

Madame Yvonne Carmeau had been storing ammunition and weapons in the fields where she operated, and when her D-Day message came, her group had to retrieve them. The plastic explosives had been buried in sacks and the weapons had been packed in soft soap before burial to prevent corroding.

THE GERMANS DISPERSED THESE VITAL FLATBEDS ON TRACKS ALL AROUND THE FRENCH COUNTRYSIDE AND CAMOUFLAGED THEM FROM AERIAL OBSERVATION. BUT IN SO DOING, THEY RAISED THE EYEBROWS OF BROOKS AND HIS SABOTEURS.

"Those were hidden under the beehives," she said. "Nobody would go and look for them there, we hoped. We had to get the beekeeper along to disturb them and the weapons were all brought out into the kitchen with the blackout on the windows, and the whole family proceeded to clean them and get all the soap off. They were ready for the next day."

Distributing the many tons of explosives was mostly via railcar where the French engineers risked their lives and hid significant amounts in obscure places on their trains. Although the Germans searched the trains, and sealed the drivers in, the game of cat-and-mouse continued. Brooks's sabotage unit had managed to accumulate thirty-three tons of plastic explosives, and most of this was sent to targeted sites by rail.

Perhaps the most obscure hiding place for explosives was a musician's tuba. "One of our main organizers in Toulouse was a tuba player," said Brooks, "and he was also secretary in the theatrical group—a great character—and he used to bring in the explosives in his tuba."

A considerable amount could fit in the cavity of the tuba. The musician bragged he could fit two British Sten guns, unassembled, into the big horn.

"It was quite a lot of explosives. He would cycle, his tuba wrapped around him as he rode, for music practice. His argument was that he had to go out into the fields to play his bloody tuba. He was a wonderful man, absolutely mad, as mad as they come."

From thousands of caches and from hundreds of cells, the resisters prepared for the oncoming battle. They would be Eisenhower's force behind German lines to stop reinforcements moving to Normandy.

Another behind-the-scenes operation was SAS. The Special Air Service (SAS) provided continuing deception about where the attack would come. Captain Michael R. D. Foot was the brigade intelligence officer.

"About three weeks before D-Day, I got the order to mount four small operations which were to assist in helping the actual detailed landing in Normandy by providing deceptions quite close to the fighting. I chose the code name for these off a list I

DOUGLAS BRINKLEY AND RONALD J. DREZ

had by me. I picked 'Titanic,' trusting that that would sound large to a German."

Foot hoped the Germans would not draw any negative conclusions about the word 'Titanic' and its connotation of disaster, and went off to see one of the regimental commanders to request four small parties to parachute into Normandy simultaneous with the main parachute drop. When Foot explained that the parties would be used for deception, the commander said no.

Foot tried one of the other regimental commanders, who agreed to provide a force, but only two teams for the D-Day insertion.

"The task of the two 'Titanic' parties was, in each case, to simulate a major airborne landing. They were accompanied by about five hundred dummy parachutists, which were supposed to self-destruct on landing with a small explosion and a flash. [The two live parties] were armed with gramophone records of soldiers' conversation interspersed with small-arms fire, and Veery pistols with masses of Veery ammunition. And they were to wander to and fro in the woods where they went down, letting off their Veery pistols and simulating major military activity."

The dummy parachutists were code-named "Rupert." In the moonlight, Rupert looked very much like a real paratrooper, and the accompanying soldiers of the SAS, firing their Veery pistols, with flashes and pyrotechnics turned the jump area into a very believable landing site.

On June 1, the droning voice on the BBC broadcast the long lists of messages. Several times during the hour between 1:30 and 2:30 p.m. it recited, "The long sobs of the violins of autumn." The German High Command heard these lines. But they had also heard them the previous month, and nothing had happened.

Four days later, June 5, the voice recited the long-awaited second line: "Wound my heart with a monotonous languor." It broadcast the line fifteen times. German General Hans von Salmuth heard it and placed his 15th Army at Pas-de-Calais on full alert. But Germany's 7th Army on the Normandy coast did not react.

Although the Germans were watchful, the diversions and sabotage carried out by the SOE, the Resistance, and the SAS made an important behind-the-scenes impact on D-Day.

Chapter

4

DROPPING FROM THE SKIES: THE BRITISH ATTACK ON THE EAST FLANK

On the morning of June 5, as Eisenhower began to visit American troops at the wharves, the British troopers led by Major John Howard repaired and straightened up their campsite at Tarrant Rushton after the terrible winds and rains from the previous night.

The dispatch rider came bicycling down for his usual rendezvous with Major Howard to whisper his one-word order. The wind was still blowing hard, and the rain was falling. Howard fully expected to receive the word that meant the invasion was not on. But the dispatch rider's word was again "Cromwell."

"We went through that day rather apprehensively expecting another cancellation," said Howard, "but we didn't get it. We loaded up the gliders, and came back, and everyone was made to rest in the afternoon. Most of us spent the time writing letters to our homes and loved ones, and left them with the military police that guarded the camp, no doubt to be censored after we left."

Howard had been assigned a remarkable mission. His force of six gliders and 180 men would be the first into France.

Disk 1, Tracks 12–16:
The British glider invasion

OPPOSITE: Shortly before takeoff, British paratroopers receive last-minute instruction. These paratroopers would rely on the success of the glider troops landing just ahead of them on D-Day.

TIME LINE	Dec. 7, 1941	Jan. 15, 1944	June 4, 1944	June 5, 1944	JUNE 6, 1944	0015–0300	0530
	Japan attacks Pearl Harbor; American enlistments increase	Eisenhower becomes supreme commander; planning intensifies	Resistance operatives in France put on D-Day alert	Eisenhower makes decision to proceed with invasion		Airborne troops land in Normandy (British to the east, then Americans to the west)	Allies bomb beaches; first ground troops land on an island off Utah Beach

British general Richard ("Windy") Gale conceived the bold plan to seize key bridges on the east flank to initiate the airborne assault on Normandy.

The idea for the daring attack began in the mind of British general Richard Gale. Everyone irresistibly called him "Windy." In 1944, Gale commanded the British 6th Airborne Division at the time General Eisenhower and his staff were fleshing out the plans for the invasion of Normandy to crack Hitler's Western Wall of Fortress Europe.

Eisenhower's plan was predominantly an amphibious assault that would storm five invasion beaches along the Normandy coast, get a foothold, and then break out to fight in the French countryside. But the success of that plan depended on getting the initial foothold.

Eisenhower had chosen the less obvious channel-crossing route, and this afforded him some surprise. But that advantage would disintegrate if the 15th Army reacted quickly and raced its forces to the west.

The Germans would then be in a position to strike Eisenhower's vulnerable left flank at Sword Beach and systematically roll up his entire force with continued flanking attacks smashing to the west along the Normandy coast. The invasion would become a nightmare of falling dominoes with failure assured as the last domino fell.

Eisenhower gave General Gale the task of preventing this dreaded flanking attack. But Gale commanded paratroopers, not armored and infantry divisions capable of withstanding a German armored thrust. Lightly armed paratroopers were least likely to stop armor, but the paratroopers were the only force capable of getting into position before the amphibious assault. Speed was the vital consideration. Once in, these lightly armed men would have to hold until relieved.

General Gale formulated his plan. He would drop his division east of Sword Beach, destroy the bridges along the Dives River ten miles farther to the east, and then set his forces in a semicircular defense behind the Dives. From there he would await his fate. The Dives would become his moat.

There was one major problem with this strategy. A canal and a river ran immediately adjacent to Sword Beach and directly behind Gale's defense. These two parallel waterways were the

DOUGLAS BRINKLEY AND RONALD J. DREZ

Caen Canal and the Orne River. Gale's force would be sandwiched between the Dives and these two bodies of water, placing him in a vulnerable position.

If the attacking German forces could destroy the bridges over the Orne River and the Caen Canal, the entire British airborne would then be isolated, fighting with its back to the water. It would be annihilated.

So General Gale conceived the idea of a strike force that would land in gliders prior to the main parachute drop. The small force would land with thunderclap surprise, and seize the two bridges, intact, before the Germans could destroy them.

It was a bold and daring plan, a plan that would certainly fail if not executed perfectly. Still, Gale thought it had a reasonable chance of success.

He reasoned that the forces defending the bridges might tend to be somewhat lethargic after having occupied northern France for four years. The Germans had been guarding lots of bridges against no opposition, and in fact had settled into an occupation mentality. Gale felt that the initial enthusiasm of conquest might have turned into boredom as night after night, year after year, guards had reported for monotonous duty where nothing ever happened.

A lightning strike could possibly seize the bridges before the defenders realized what was happening. Intelligence reports indicated that the bridges were wired for demolition: but were the detonation wires kept hooked to the hellbox that would trigger the detonation? Most likely not. The bridge commander would not risk an accidental explosion.

And when the attack commenced, surely the German guards would not blow the bridge at the first shot. There would be several minutes of indecision. The guards would first try to determine what was happening. There would be hell to pay for anyone who blew the bridges because of a knee-jerk reaction to some minor armed disturbance.

Adding up all of his suppositions, General Gale estimated that he had five minutes to get to the bridges and disarm them before the defenders could put two and two together. If the attack took

LIGHTLY ARMED PARATROOPERS WERE LEAST LIKELY TO STOP ARMOR, BUT THE PARATROOPERS WERE THE ONLY FORCE CAPABLE OF GETTING INTO POSITION BEFORE THE AMPHIBIOUS ASSAULT. SPEED WAS THE VITAL CONSIDERATION. ONCE IN, THESE LIGHTLY ARMED MEN WOULD HAVE TO HOLD UNTIL RELIEVED.

THE PLAN WAS FOR THREE GLIDERS UNDER HOWARD TO LAND AND SEIZE THE BRIDGE ON THE CAEN CANAL (WHICH CAME TO BE CALLED "PEGASUS BRIDGE") WHILE THE REMAINING THREE GLIDERS UNDER CAPTAIN PRIDAY WOULD SEIZE THE PARALLEL BRIDGE OVER THE ORNE RIVER FOUR HUNDRED YARDS AWAY.

longer than five minutes, Gale assumed, the bridges would not be seized intact.

To lead a force that would have to squeeze this successful attack into a five-minute window, Gale and his planners chose Major John Howard and his Company D, Oxfordshire and Buckinghamshire Light Infantry Regiment. Howard was allowed to reinforce his four platoons with two additional platoons from Company B, along with thirty sappers from the Royal Engineers. This force would forever after be known as "Company D, Ox and Bucks."

Many called John Howard's force the most elite troops in the British Army. One umpire who participated in the training exercises watched as the Ox and Bucks men hurled themselves onto barbed wire barricades so that those following behind could use them as stepping-stones over the obstacle. Sergeant Tich Raynor watched one umpire shaking his head, muttering, "I pity the bloody Germans; these buggers are mad!"

John Howard's second-in-command was a dashingly good-looking captain named Brian Priday. The plan was for three gliders under Howard to land and seize the bridge on the Caen Canal (which came to be called "Pegasus Bridge") while the remaining three gliders under Captain Priday would seize the parallel bridge over the Orne River four hundred yards away.

Now the day was at hand. The order had been given, and Howard and his men would lead the force into France.

"Come nine o'clock as had been planned," said Howard, "we got into our troop-carrying vehicles, and the wind seemed to be quite as bad as it had been, and there was rain in the air, and God knows what, except the sky seemed to be clearing. By the time we were to get into the gliders, you could see a half-moon. We were up by the gliders by ten o'clock, and everyone went to check equipment."

Howard went to each of his men and shook their hands and gave a farewell slap on the back and exchanged their "Ham and Jam" farewell.

"Those words were code words and they meant a terrible lot to us in that transit camp," explained Howard. "They were the success-signal code words for the capture of the bridges intact. There were various code words for if you captured the river bridge, blown-up, or you didn't capture it at all—the same for the canal bridge. The success-signal for the canal bridge was 'Ham,' and for the river bridge, 'Jam.' And it was a goodwill wish for everyone—'Ham and Jam.'"

The words no one mentioned were the code words for failure to seize both bridges. No one mentioned "Jack" and "Lard."

Howard and his men settled in on the canvas sling seats in the Horsa glider, after making sure the towropes were properly fastened to the Halifax bombers that would tow them across the channel.

"I then took my seat in the #1 glider," said Howard. "This was Den Brotheridge's platoon. I was opposite the opened door and on my right was two other men and then the cockpit. I could look through to the cockpit and see Staff Sergeant Jim Wallwork, the pilot, quite clearly. We shut the doors, and my glider was due to take off at 2256, and it started onto the runway with a Halifax bomber towing it and right on the dot at 2256 it was airborne, and although I couldn't see them, I knew that the rest of the five were in line right behind us."

Behind Glider #1 the rest of the force was indeed in line being towed into the sky by other bombers. In Glider #2 was Lieutenant David Wood's platoon, #3—Lieutenant Sandy Smith's. These three gliders would hopefully land in a position to attack the bridge over the Caen Canal.

Captain Brian Priday was in Glider #4 with Lieutenant Tony Hooper's platoon, followed by Glider #5 with Tod Sweeney's, and Glider #6 with Dennis Fox's. These last three gliders would try to land and seize the bridge over the Orne River.

"We were cut off from the rest of the world except for Jim Wallwork's ability to talk to the Halifax," said John Howard. "Through the portholes we could see lots of other bombers, and we knew they must have been going to bomb the invasion front. We knew that we would be just over an hour in the air crossing the Channel."

Major John Howard led the first troops into Normandy in a stealthy, glider-borne assault.

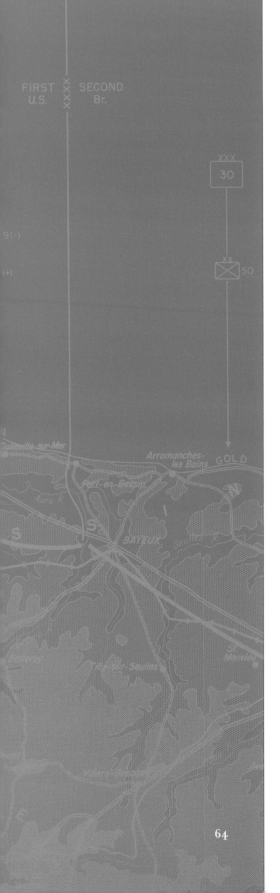

The flight plan called for Howard's force to cross the French coastline at the seaside town of Cabourg, about ten miles east of the bridges and the east edge of the invasion area. Once the gliders freed themselves from their tows, the bombers would continue on their own mission to bomb the city of Caen.

The bombing would provide a diversion for the silent gliders, which would then stretch their glides in ever decreasing circles to reach the bridges. Flying upwind, downwind, and crosswind legs, each pilot would navigate to the landing area with only compass and stopwatch. During the approach, he would try to pick out the structure of the Caen Canal bridge and then land by the light of the half-moon.

The landing was fraught with danger. For it to be successful, the pilots had to bring their powerless machines to a halt intact and within a very short distance from the bridge. In the back of each man's mind was the unthinkable: crashing and splintering, killing all aboard.

And what about the Germans? Had they sown the field with "Rommel's Asparagus"? That's what everyone called the telephone poles that Rommel had ordered installed to rip the wings off gliders and thus prevent airborne landings. These obstacles had suddenly appeared in recent aerial photos where they had not been seen weeks before. All this was in John Howard's mind as he droned on to the French coast and his release point over the town of Cabourg.

"At the last minute I was wondering what the strength of the enemy would be when we pranged, because we had that trouble about Rommel's poles, and I was worried about the question of a machine gun pointing toward one glider wiping us all out altogether in one fell swoop before we could have a chance to fight back. I also was concerned about the explosives which we carried in the glider and whether they would explode on landing."

Staff Sergeants Jim Wallwork and John Ainsworth were in the cockpit of Glider #1. Wallwork was the pilot. As they approached the French coast, he saw the shoreline through the broken clouds.

Captain Brian Priday (center),
John Howard's second-in-command,
was to lead the troops from Gliders
number 4, 5, and 6.

He had the only radio communication in the glider to speak to the bomber pilot.

"We had just hit the coast of France," Wallwork said, "and the tug pilot said, 'Weather's good, the clouds are at six thousand feet, a couple of minutes before we cast off, and we all wish you the best of luck.'

"We alter course, air speed's right, John Ainsworth's with the stopwatch; I'm checking the compass, he's checking the air speed. We cruise along and then 5-4-3-2-1, bingo, right turn to starboard onto course."

The big glider made the ninety-degree turn to starboard, and again Ainsworth started the stopwatch to begin timing the glide for the crosswind leg of the flight. But Wallwork did not complete the crosswind leg.

"I COULD SEE THE BRIDGES;
VISIBILITY WAS AWFULLY
GOOD. SO THEN, TO HELL
WITH THE COURSE; I KNEW
MY HEIGHT; I KNEW HOW
FAR AWAY I WAS, SO IT WAS
A CASE OF BY GUESS AND
BY GOD FROM THEN ON.
I DIDN'T COMPLETE THE
CROSSWIND LEG, SO
I BOWLED DOWN AND
LANDED RATHER QUICKLY."

—GLIDER PILOT JIM WALLWORK

"Halfway down the crosswind leg, I could see it," said the excited pilot. "I could see the river and the canal-like strips of silver, and I could see the bridges; visibility was awfully good. So then, to hell with the course; I knew my height; I knew how far away I was, so it was a case of by guess and by God from then on. I didn't complete the crosswind leg, so I bowled down and landed rather quickly."

The men in the glider felt the aircraft descending and went into their pre-landing routine. Each man linked arms with the man on either side of him, locked his own hands in front of himself, and lifted his feet off the floor since it most likely would disintegrate.

Howard could look to his right and see Wallwork maneuvering the glider. He could not see the landing area or anything but the pilot working the controls.

"I could see old Jim holding that bloody great machine and driving it in at the last minute," said Howard. "I couldn't see his face, but I could see those damn great footballs of sweat across his forehead and all over his face, and I felt for him and was holding that damn thing myself as we came in."

The ideal landing speed for the Horsa glider was 85 mph, but Glider #1 was coming in hot. Wallwork saw the small triangular field, and he could see the superstructure of the bridge, and barbed wire, and he struggled to get the glider down.

"There was a feeling of the land rushing up," he said, "and I landed probably at about ninety-five instead of at eighty-five, and ten miles per hour in the dark looks like a lot. I hit the field and caught the first bit of wire and so I called 'Stream' and by golly, it [the parachute] lifted the tail and forced the nose down. It drew us back and knocked the speed down tremendously. It was only on for two seconds and, 'Jettison,' and Ainsworth pressed the tit and jettisoned the parachute, and then we were going along only about sixty, which was ample to take me right into the corner. We got right into the corner of the field, the nose wheel had gone, the cockpit collapsed, and Ainsworth and I went right through the cockpit. I went over head first and landed flat on my stomach. I was stunned, as was Ainsworth."

DOUGLAS BRINKLEY AND RONALD J. DREZ

Howard had been tossed about. He picked himself up from what remained of the floor of the glider. The front of the glider had telescoped and the door was nowhere to be seen, and Howard suddenly realized that he could not see.

"But I was, in a semiconscious sort of way, aware that I had banged my head, and when I realized it was only the helmet down over my eyes, I was able to lever it up and see clearly, and the relief of knowing that I hadn't hit my head badly was tremendous. My watch had stopped at 0016, and then the exhilaration of seeing the tower of the bridge in that moonlight was an extraordinary thing. There it was, about fifty yards away from where we were."

The nose of the glider was through the barbed wire, and the troopers silently gathered for the attack. Howard watched the section leaders form up their units at the slope leading to the bridge. Lieutenant Brotheridge was in charge, giving Corporal Jack Bailey whispered instructions.

Major John Howard (leaning against the plane) and Staff Sergeant Jim Wallwork (standing) flew together in Glider #1. Wallwork piloted this lead glider, which came in hard and fast.

"When we got out of the glider, Den Brotheridge whispered to me, 'Corporal Bailey, get those chaps moving.' And we moved, and we streamed across the road. The task of our section was to neutralize the pillbox. We scrambled across and the ironwork of the bridge stood out like a great black silhouette. We went straight to the pillbox and used two '36 grenades,' Wally Parr and myself, which we put through the apertures, and there was a terrific explosion."

Parr had overcome his initial fright and attacked with Corporal Bailey.

"I ran up the incline onto the bridge and looked. For some reason, I just looked at everything, and my tongue was stuck to the roof of my mouth and I couldn't spit six-pence. My mouth had dried up of all saliva. I couldn't free it and I finally shouted, "Come out and fight, you square-headed bastards."

As Lieutenant Brotheridge led the attack, Gliders #2 and #3 arrived in the small field. Staff Sergeant Oliver Boland piloted #2. As he wrestled the glider down, he could see that he was going to land a little short of his target.

"I stretched the glide as far as I could as the bridges came into view, and I was now quite low. Suddenly there was gunfire right in front of my nose, and we then, literally, crash-landed. I had to keep to Wallwork's right, otherwise I'd have run up his bum, and I used the spoilers and dropped the last foot or so and, *Bash!* And then I see another bloke coming in from my right, which was the third glider. So I dropped on the ground with an almighty crash, and we crashed along and managed to stop."

Glider #3 frantically tried to put down safely. Glider #2 had landed a little short in the small field, greatly reducing the space for #3 to put down. Lieutenant Sandy Smith was the platoon commander.

"I saw the bridge as we passed over it and came around in a great big sweep, and then as we started to come close to the ground, the pilot said, 'You'd better sit down.' Then we hit this, what I call a slop swamp, and there was a very large bounce as we hit the ground, and I knew we were in trouble."

The glider became airborne again.

"There were several seconds between that first bounce and then the most amazing, appalling crash. I went shooting straight past these two pilots; I shot out like a bullet and landed in front of the glider."

The glider had hit with such force that it broke in half by a small pond in the field. One of the men was thrown into the pond and pinned underwater by one of the wings. Glider #3 finally came to rest between #1 and #2, narrowly missing destroying two-thirds of the landing force.

"I staggered to my feet," said Smith. "I lost my Sten gun, and I staggered by instinct toward the bridge, followed by not more than a half a dozen people. The rest were trapped in the glider, and one of my chaps, Higgs, was drowned in it—the doctor was knocked unconscious."

Smith arrived just a few minutes after the troops from Glider #1 had launched their attack. Already they had secured the bridge and driven off the defenders. But not without cost. Smith remembers:

"Seconds later someone came up to me and said, 'Mr. Brotheridge is dead, sir.'"

Major John Howard had set up his command post on the other side across the road from the gliders. Knowing the canal bridge was now in his hands, he turned toward the river bridge just four hundred yards down the road.

"I wondered what the devil was happening over on the river bridge," said Howard. "I could see no firing on the river bridge, so I knew that they didn't have to fight for the bridge, but I didn't even know if they had arrived there because I kept asking the radio operator, Tappenden, was there anything from the river, from [Glider] 4, 5, or 6, and the answer was, 'No, no, no.' And it was at that junction that Jock Neilson came up to me and said, 'There are no explosives under the bridge, John.' We eventually found them in a shed farther down past the pillbox.

"Just then Corporal Tappenden picked up a message from #6. Nothing from 4 or 5, but #6—Dennis Fox. His message was that they'd captured the bridge without firing a shot. Well that was tremendous news to get."

Corporal Jack Bailey (left) and Wally Parr (center) landed with Glider #1 and were among the first to charge the bridges. The third man pictured is Harry Woodthorpe.

Glider #6 had made a perfect landing, skidding along on its belly to a smooth stop. Lieutenant Dennis Fox's first problem came in just trying to get out of the glider.

"I could not open the door for the love of money," said Fox. "I pulled and pulled and pulled, and good old Sergeant Wagger Thornton came up from the back and said, 'You just pull it forward, sir,' and then up it lifted and we jumped out."

Fox led the way across the field toward the bridge and suddenly received a burst of automatic fire.

"It was a Schmizzer [a German machine gun], and dear old Thornton from way back had gotten from his position a mortar going, and he put a mortar slap down on that gun—a fabulous shot."

Fox had the bridge, and moments later troopers from #6 arrived under Lieutenant Tod Sweeney, who charged across the opposite end toward Dennis Fox.

"I went racing over with these chaps all thumping along beside me," said Sweeney, "and when we got to the far side there were clearly British figures. We came to a halt, and, I must say, rather disappointedly—we'd been all worked up—and there was the unmistakable figure of Dennis Fox."

Both bridges had been taken intact. General Gale's plan had worked. The Ox and Bucks had a toehold in France. Now they had to hold on.

"We were able immediately to start sending out our 'Ham and Jam' radio call," said Howard. But try as he might, Corporal Tappenden could not raise a soul on his wireless.

He transmitted over and over. "Hello, Four Dog; Hello, Four Dog, Ham and Jam, Ham and Jam!" He paused for an answer, but there was only silence on the airwaves.

"For a solid hour I lay on that road," said Tappenden. "I finally got so frustrated that I said, 'Hello, Four Dog; Hello, Four Dog, *Ham and Jam, Ham and Bloody Jam*, why don't you answer me?'"

The first Germans to approach Howard's position came from the east toward the river bridge, unaware of the British presence. A small patrol and, later, a speeding Mercedes came across the bridge, both easily dispatched by Company D.

DOUGLAS BRINKLEY AND RONALD J. DREZ

But at 2 a.m., two tanks approached the T-junction a hundred yards west of the canal bridge.

"We could see them moving very, very slowly about twenty-five yards apart," said Howard, "obviously not knowing what to expect when they got down to the bridges. The only weapons I had to stop them were the PIATs [Projector Infantry Anti-Tank]. It was a spring-fired weapon and it fired a bomb about a foot long. It had a very high trajectory."

Sergeant Wagger Thornton from the #6 platoon was chosen to be the gunner.

"The tanks were making their way down probably to recapture the bridge, and Howard asked Fox if he had a PIAT, and I suddenly found myself entrusted with the PIAT. I took a chap with me, to be a number two, and off we went. Now a PIAT is a load of rubbish really. First, you're a dead loss if you have to go even fifty yards, and second you must never, never, miss. If you do, you've had it because by the time you reload the thing and cock it, which is a chore on its own, everything is gone. You're indoctrinated into your brain that you mustn't miss. So, I lay down with this other guy about thirty yards from the T-junction of the road. I was shaking like a bloody leaf. Sure enough, in about three minutes this bloody thing appears, the old wheels were rattling away, and I could more hear it than see it. I took an aim, and although shaking, *bang*, and off it went. The thing exploded right bang in the middle, and a couple of minutes later, all hell let loose. I was so excited and shaking, and I had to move back a bit. Two or three guys jumped out of the thing, and I said to my number two to give them a few bursts from the Sten, which he did."

Howard was jubilant. Thornton had destroyed the tank that could have kicked his force off the bridge and jeopardized the entire operation. Once the first tank exploded, the second tank beat a hasty retreat. But Howard's jubilation was tempered by the fact that Glider #4 had not landed. One-sixth of his force was presumed lost.

In fact, Glider #4 was not lost. It was very much in a fight of its own. The pilot had become disoriented and flew in a great circle, finally spotting a silver stream of water reflected in the light of the half-moon.

BOTH BRIDGES HAD BEEN TAKEN INTACT. GENERAL GALE'S PLAN HAD WORKED. THE OX AND BUCKS HAD A TOEHOLD IN FRANCE. NOW THEY HAD TO HOLD ON.

OPPOSITE: The successful seizure of the bridge over the Caen Canal (Pegasus Bridge), and the nearby bridge over the Orne River, had established the toehold necessary for the British airborne to secure the area. Shown here on June 7, Allied troops roll across Pegasus Bridge, the wreckage of two gliders visible in the background.

He made his approach and set the glider down smooth as velvet on the left bank of the river. "We had a very comfortable, soft landing in the water on the riverbank," said Lance Corporal Felix Clive. "We got out and were only fifty yards from the bridge, and Captain Priday led the way."

"We rushed the bridge," said Lance Sergeant Tich Raynor, "and we took the bridge. There was a German sentry there and he ran away. He left his helmet on the parapet of the bridge and ran."

The bridge was secured, but it was the wrong bridge. Priday's men had seized a bridge along the Dives River about ten miles from the objective bridges. Lieutenant Hooper immediately went off toward the right, down the road in the direction of the invasion area. Captain Priday split his force so that half were on each end of their bridge on the Dives.

But shortly, German fire came from Hooper's direction and one shot hit the wireless operator in the head, killing him instantly. And then, from the same direction, Raynor and Priday could see dark figures approaching. The troopers flattened themselves into the grass on the shoulder of the embankment.

In the moonlight, they could make out the familiar figure of Lieutenant Hooper. But he was not walking confidently. He had his boots tied around his neck, his hands were over his head, and he marched in front of a German soldier who had his automatic pistol trained on Hooper's back.

Raynor was on one side of the road and Priday was on the other. When Hooper and the German were only ten yards from them, they shouted out together, "Jump, Tony!"

Hooper jumped into the ditch away from the German, and as he jumped, Raynor and Priday opened fire. Each emptied a full magazine. Several of the others also fired, and the German went down. As he fell, he pulled the trigger and held it in his death grip. The automatic fired in a loud burp. The spray of bullets cut Priday's map case in half, and one bullet tore into Sergeant Raynor's arm.

The following morning Captain Priday started his men off across enemy-held territory to work his way to Major Howard. Escaping and evading enemy forces, he finally arrived in the early hours of June 7 to greet a surprised and happy John Howard.

DOUGLAS BRINKLEY AND RONALD J. DREZ

OVER THE ATLANTIC WALL: THE AMERICAN AIRBORNE DROP ON THE COTENTIN PENINSULA

Shortly after the Halifax bombers took off with John Howard's Ox and Bucks, 822 C-47 Dakota aircraft loaded their paratroopers at scattered airfields in southern England. At Greenham Common, Membury, Merryfield, North Witham, Uppottery, Exeter, and Aldermaston, more than thirteen thousand overloaded paratroopers with blackened faces pushed and pulled and tugged and shoved each other and their bulging packs into the cramped spaces of the aircraft that would ferry them to the French countryside. Some paratroopers carried loads over 150 pounds.

Each planeload was called a "stick," consisting of sixteen to twenty-three men. They sat in sling seats along either side of the C-47, facing inboard, and overhead, running down the length of the fuselage, was the static line. When it came time to jump, the pilot would turn on a red light, signaling the troopers to stand in the aisle, back to front, and snap their D rings onto the static line. Then the order to check equipment and "Count off!"

Disk 1, Tracks 17–21: The U.S. Airborne invasion

OPPOSITE: Paratroopers of the 82nd Airborne Division drop from C-47s during training exercises.

TIME LINE	Dec. 7, 1941	Jan. 15, 1944	June 4, 1944	June 5, 1944	JUNE 6, 1944	0015–0300	0530
	Japan attacks Pearl Harbor; American enlistments increase	Eisenhower becomes supreme commander; planning intensifies	Resistance operatives in France put on D-Day alert	Eisenhower makes decision to proceed with invasion		Airborne troops land in Normandy (British to the east, then Americans to the west)	Allies bomb beaches; first ground troops land on an island off Utah Beach

0630	0700	0730–0745	0930–1330	1203	1300	1600	2400
H-Hour on Utah and Omaha Beaches	U.S. Army Rangers scale Pointe du Hoc	H-Hour on Gold, Sword, and Juno Beaches	Troops advance inland	British commandos meet airborne troops at Orne bridges	U.S. 4th Infantry meets 101st Airborne at Pouppeville	Tanks move inland from Omaha Beach	Five beach-heads secured; liberation under way

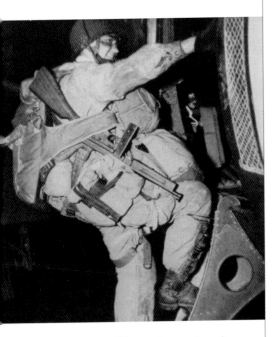

An Airborne trooper boards his plane en route to Normandy.

From the rear of the aircraft, the last man would shout out, "Sixteen, OK," and the count would proceed forward to number one. All that remained was for the light to turn from red to green, and the troopers would plunge out into the night air over Normandy.

The exiting paratroopers would shuffle and hip-hop forward, staying pressed tightly to one another so as to exit in a tight unit to avoid scattering upon landing. On the ground, the men would close upon the center man in a maneuver called "rolling up the stick." Hopefully, within a short time, a sixteen-man fighting force would have assembled, ready to fight.

"There would be twenty 'serials,' fifteen miles apart," said Lieutenant Carl Cartledge. "The first ten would be the 101st Airborne Division, the second would be the 82nd Airborne, 13,400 paratroopers in all, and in an armada three hundred miles long, nine planes wide, flying in three Vs and at altitudes from seven thousand to five hundred feet. We would be parachuting down into France from 12:30 a.m. to 2:30 a.m. on six drop zones, each one mile long and a half mile wide."

At Greenham Commons, paratrooper Ken Cordry stood in formation while General Eisenhower visited them.

"We assembled in formation while General Eisenhower walked through the ranks, talking with many of the men. He talked to troopers like me, but I wasn't one of the lucky ones. I really felt, after hearing him, that he was really concerned about our safety and our chances of surviving the invasion drop."

Elvy Roberts, an assistant platoon commander with the 101st, boarded his plane. His group felt pretty cocky. Although they had all been drafted into the army, they had all volunteered to be paratroopers.

"We started taxiing out around 10:30. I remember standing in the door looking at this tremendous armada of airplanes. It was tremendously impressive. I was very proud to be a platoon leader, it was something that we had trained and worked for. They had painted the stripes on the airplanes. We knew where we were going that night when we saw the planes with the stripes on them."

DOUGLAS BRINKLEY AND RONALD J. DREZ

Paratroopers of the 101st Airborne Division took on intimidating visages, giving each other mohawk haircuts and painting their faces. Seen here is a photo captured from a rare film of the preparations.

The black and white stripes became known as "invasion stripes," and all aircraft had suddenly appeared with these stripes on their wings and fuselages. They would ensure positive identification of an Allied airplane. Anything without stripes was the enemy.

In the darkness of the June 5 night, the great sky train roared down the runways for the assault on the western flank of the invasion area. Like the British airborne on the eastern flank, the American airborne was to provide flank security on the west, especially security for the four narrow causeways that led from Utah Beach across flooded lowland. The objective of the 101st Airborne was the town of Carentan and its surroundings. The 82nd was to secure the critical town of Sainte-Mère-Église. Through these two towns, most of the major roads passed.

At this exact time, the German High Command, Oberbefehlshaber West (OB West), and 15th Army each intercepted coded messages that announced that the invasion would occur within forty-eight hours. The 15th Army, at Pas-de-Calais, immediately put its troops on the highest alert. But Army Group B, in charge of forces at Normandy, took no action. The giant sky train would approach Normandy while German forces were sleeping.

On June 5, 1944, General Eisenhower visited with the paratroopers of the 101st Airborne Division just before they boarded their planes.

"The flight in was uneventful," said Roberts, "except for one or two who had gotten airsick. At first there was some singing, and then everyone was tired: most slept. It quieted down soon after we got started. We did a course straight south and then cut back to the east.

"As the air armada approached the peninsula from west to east, the Germans put up a tremendous volume of antiaircraft fire.

"I was standing in the door and I could see planes being hit. My platoon leader's plane was lost. That's the way it was. As we progressed farther, the 20mm and the 40mm antiaircraft became

DOUGLAS BRINKLEY AND RONALD J. DREZ

more and more intense. I could see the streams like a water hose of fire coming up and the stream of tracers."

Sherman Oyler was the number one man in his plane carrying members of the 502nd PIR. On the flight over the channel he reflected on his unique conversation with General Eisenhower.

"I had just wanted to see General Eisenhower, and had no idea that he would talk with me," said Oyler. "When he came up, he asked me, 'What is your name, soldier?' Well, I drew a blank and I couldn't remember my name, and I kept saying to myself, 'What is my name? What is my name? What is my name?' Finally some of the guys hollered, 'Well, tell him your name, Oyler!' Then he asked me what my hometown was, and when I said, 'Wellington, Kansas,' he said, 'Oh, that's south of Wichita.'"

Eisenhower then gave his famous thumbs-up just as a cameraman snapped the picture, and said, "Go, Kansas."

Now Oyler was in the number one position on his C-47 over France. As his plane started its descent from fifteen hundred feet down to seven hundred feet for the jump, the aircraft was vibrating from one end to the other. The German fire was everywhere, and then the C-47 entered a cloud bank which made it almost impossible to see the drop zones.

"After what seemed an eternity," said Oyler, "the red light flashed on inside the plane. Everyone stood up and hooked up. I helped get the door bundles ready to push out, when one of the troopers was hit in the rear by pieces of flak, and a medic and a trooper had him drop his pants and they dressed his wounds."

The air over the drop zones was thick with flak and antiaircraft fire. All the paratroopers stared out of windows to see the flashes and tracers.

"It sounds like rocks in a tin can when the bullets hit the aircraft," said Lieutenant Carl Cartledge of the 501st PIR, 101st Airborne. "No one had to tell us what it was when we heard it for the first time. The light of the tracers was partially blinding the pilots."

"I was looking over the shoulders of the men in front of me," said Leland Baker. "I was about halfway to the end of the stick, and the light turned green. We all filed out the door. My chute

THE AIR OVER THE DROP ZONES WAS THICK WITH FLAK AND ANTIAIRCRAFT FIRE. ALL THE PARATROOPERS STARED OUT OF WINDOWS TO SEE THE FLASHES AND TRACERS.

The paratroopers piled into the C-47 Dakota aircraft in "sticks" of sixteen to twenty-three men. Some troopers carried over 150 pounds.

jerked me so hard that I reared back and looked up to see if I'd blown any panels. When I did, there was a string of tracers that went through my canopy."

Parachutes filled the air over the Cotentin Peninsula as the troopers from the 101st and 82nd descended toward earth. The startled French gazed into the air at the strange sight. Many called it the "night of the little mushrooms."

The first four men in the aircraft with Leonard Griffing jumped into the night—then there was trouble for the rest of the stick.

"When it was time to stand up and hook up," said Griffing, "most of us were so airsick that jumping out seemed a reasonable thing to do. At least it was better than staying.

"I was pretty far forward in the stick, maybe number four or five, and I could see out the doorway. The sky was lighted up

DOUGLAS BRINKLEY AND RONALD J. DREZ

with tracers. I remember seeing one of the transports off a quarter mile get hit and explode, just a big ball of flame.

"As I stood there with my hands on the edge of the doorway ready to push out, it seemed that we took some kind of a burst under the left wing, because the plane went in a sharp roll and I couldn't push myself out because it was uphill, so I just hung on. The rest of the stick tried to hang on to the jump cable, but they either fell or almost fell.

"The pilot got ahold of the ship, stopped the roll and started rolling it back the other way. As soon as he got it to where I could push myself out, I did, and I was in the air. The guy that went out before me was a half-mile behind us. And by the time the guy behind me got out, he was a half-mile away from me in the other direction. My chute popped open and I was the only parachute in the sky.

"The moon had gone behind the cloud, and it was so dark that I had no idea what I was landing on. It could have been grass, might have been trees, could have been water. Also, what was below me and what I seemed to be coming down on top of was four muzzle blasts that I could see following me all the way down."

The problems facing the troop carrier pilots were enormous. Night flying, flak, cloud banks, and the sheer numbers of planes maneuvering in the air made for a harrowing experience. The flak was terrifying.

"The sky was filled with red and green tracers," said Lieutenant Sidney Ulan of the 99th Troop Carrier Squadron (TCS), "and searchlights beamed up at the planes just ahead of me. The saliva in my mouth completely dried up from the fright."

Lieutenant Roger Airgood was a veteran troop carrier aviator. But despite all his training, the Normandy night drop was overwhelming.

"Although we experienced many night formations with paratroopers in the States and in England, the plan for getting the troops to the drop zones in Normandy was the most complex and ambitious mission we had ever faced," he said.

"Everything was working fine as scheduled until we got to the last light boat [in the English Channel], at which time we

Sidney M. Ulan was a pilot in the 99th Troop Carrier Squadron, which dropped paratroopers into Normandy on D-Day. This picture of him was taken in the summer of 1944.

This photo shows some members of the 501st Parachute Infantry Regiment, 101st Airborne Division, with the camouflaged parachutes they would use in Normandy.

were to turn off the amber down light and reduce the formation lights to half power. Hays, the pilot flying on [Lieutenant Colonel] Kreyssler's left, turned down the formation lights so low they were not visible. Hays could see nothing of Kreyssler's wingman from the left seat, so I flew from the right seat since I could see the exhaust stack glow and the phantom outline of the plane. We maintained the course, and when coming out of a cloud bank, we could see tracers coming up from many angles. The lines of tracers arched over us as we flew under them. There was a tremendous racket such as experienced when flying through hail. I had very few glimpses of the ground since I had to keep the outline of the plane in sight. Shortly after getting the four-minute red warning light, I got a glimpse of a steeple of a church about a half-mile ahead and off to the right about a quarter of a mile. Assuming this to be Sainte-Mère-Église, I felt we were on course and that DZ A [Drop Zone A] lay straight ahead.

"There seemed to be a delay in slowing down to the jump speed of 110 mph. When Kreyssler did slow down, it was too fast. Wingmen had to cut power and hold the nose up to keep from overrunning the lead planes, which in turn was followed by a blast of power to keep the plane from stalling out. The net result was that when we got the green light, we were flying about 105 mph and pulling a lot of power. The paratroopers went out in a terrific prop blast, which was the last thing we wanted to happen."

DOUGLAS BRINKLEY AND RONALD J. DREZ

Lieutenant Airgood's experience was common in the sky train of 822 C-47s. What was worse was the effect on the paratroopers inside the aircraft. As planes sped up and slowed down and took evasive action, the troopers were standing in the aircraft. The rolling and pitching knocked them down and tossed them around like so much loose cargo. They were weaving and staggering in the aisles. When the green light flashed on, some men were still struggling to their feet; some in the front of the plane had jumped, while the remainder were delayed because of someone down on the floor. By the time the rest exited, there was major scattering that translated to wide dispersion on the ground.

James Eads was the sixteenth man in his plane. "Our C-47 had been hit at the worst time by both flak and machine-gun fire," said Eads. "We were off target. The green light came on and the troopers started out of the plane, but the fifteenth man had equipment trouble. After some delay trying to fix his rig, I, being the sixteenth and last man to go out, bailed out on a dead run. My opening shock was terrific."

"We start picking up flak, light at first," said Private Dwayne Burns of the 508th PIR. "We crossed the coastline and it got heavier as we stood waiting for the green light. Now the ship's being hit from all sides. The noise is awesome. The roar of the engines, the flak hitting the wings and fuselage, and everyone is yelling, 'Let's go!' But still the green light does not come on. The ship is bouncing like something gone wild. I can hear a ticking sound as machine-gun rounds walk across the wings. It's hard to stand up, and troopers are falling down and getting up; some are getting sick. Of all the training we had, there was not anything that prepared us for this."

Perhaps the worst experience was Sergeant Dan Furlong's. "You could see the shells coming up," he said. "They looked like Roman candles. We were hit three times. There were three in the plane that got killed and four wounded.

"I was assistant jump master, who always jumps last. There were eighteen of us in the plane and the guys that were killed were probably numbers four, five, and six. The first shell hit the

Private Dwayne T. Burns jumped into Normandy with the 508th Parachute Infantry Regiment, 82nd Airborne Division.

Lieutenant Carl Cartledge was #1 Team Leader, Regimental Intelligence and Reconnaissance Section (S2), 501st Parachute Infantry Regiment, 101st Airborne Division. He is shown here just before boarding for Normandy.

wing. It took about three feet off of the tip. The next one hit right alongside the door and took the light panel off. The next one went through the floor and it blew a hole about two feet across the floor and then hit the ceiling and exploded in the plane.

"There was so much confusion in there you didn't know what was going on, because there was smoke, and static lines and parachutes all over inside that airplane. The lieutenant was waiting for the lights to come on and I was telling him to jump. The pilot was telling us to jump, because the pilot knew the lights were gone anyway.

"When I went out there was a wounded guy lying on the floor, and I fell in the hole in the floor before I got to the door, and there were static lines already hooked up, and there were chutes open in the plane. You had to get through all this to get to the door. The chutes from the guys who were killed were opened because they fell down hooked up and partially pulled them out. Then I dove out the door. Don't ask me how I got out, but I dove, head first!"

On the ground, American paratroopers began their war in the dark. Some stumbled around never finding anyone; others teamed up with buddies or with troopers they did not know. Some found themselves neck-deep in water, struggling for their lives as they landed out of their drop zones in flooded areas.

Tom Porcella of the 82nd Airborne made a watery landing. "I plunged into water. My heart was pounding and my thoughts were running a mile a minute. 'How deep is this water? Can I get free of my chute? Am I too heavy? Will the weight keep me on the bottom?'

"The water was just above my nose. I stood on my toes and was gasping for another breath of air, and my heart was beating so rapidly that I thought it would burst. I pleaded, 'Oh, God. Please don't let me drown in this damn water in the middle of nowhere.'

"I tried to remove the leg straps, but they were just too tight and it wouldn't unsnap. I needed some more air, so I jumped up and as soon as my head was above water I began splashing around. I started to pray standing on my toes with my head barely above water; my heart was beating faster. After a few seconds, I calmed down and decided to cut the straps.

"'God, my only chance is the knife. Please let it be there.' Going down into the water again, I felt for my right boot. Yes, my knife was still there. I'm lucky. I removed the knife from the sheath, and jumped up for more air, and then went below the water and slipped it in between the leg and the strap, working it back and forth in an upward motion. Nothing happened. I was in a panic. I came up for another breath of air and I thought my heart was going to burst with fright. I wanted to scream for help but I knew that would make matters worse. I told myself, 'I must think. Think! Why can't I cut the strap, my knife is razor sharp?' As I was gasping for air, I kept on saying Hail Marys. It seemed an eternity before I realized I had the blade upside down."

Carl Cartledge drifted down from plane #44. In the moonlight he could see the silvery reflection of water.

"There was water everywhere below," he said, "except just a small strip that I could see, and I was drifting dangerously close to the water. I pushed my thumbs into the saddle of the chute and sat down and quickly unbuckled my leg straps, preparing for a water landing. I was working on my chest straps when my shoe caught a small tree and I smashed into marshy ground."

Cartledge tried to get out of his chute and then move toward the center of the drop line to make contact with the rest of the stick.

"I got out of my chute with my knife and moved forward to John Fordik," he said, "then to Smith who was struggling to walk, and Bravo joined us along the way. We helped Smith on forward until we reached the number thirteen man at the river's edge as it turned inward into a wide expanse of water. There was no sound from the water. It was obvious to us the first twelve men of plane #44 had drowned."

In Company F of the 505th PIR, the red light came on, and soon turned green. Lieutenant Harold Cadish was the first man out. Hip-hopping forward, the entire stick jumped for their drop zone. Sergeant John Ray, the platoon sergeant, was the last one to exit the aircraft. The objective of the 82nd Airborne was to

"THE SHIP'S BEING HIT FROM ALL SIDES. THE NOISE IS AWESOME. THE ROAR OF THE ENGINES, THE FLAK HITTING THE WINGS AND FUSELAGE, AND EVERYONE IS YELLING, 'LET'S GO!' BUT STILL THE GREEN LIGHT DOES NOT COME ON."
—PRIVATE DWAYNE BURNS

ON THE GROUND, AMERICAN
PARATROOPERS BEGAN THEIR
WAR IN THE DARK. SOME
STUMBLED AROUND NEVER
FINDING ANYONE; OTHERS
TEAMED UP WITH BUDDIES
OR TROOPERS THEY DID
NOT KNOW. SOME FOUND
THEMSELVES NECK-DEEP IN
WATER, STRUGGLING FOR
THEIR LIVES AS THEY
LANDED OUT OF THEIR DROP
ZONES IN FLOODED AREAS.

seize the crossroads town of Sainte-Mère-Église. The drop zones were to the northwest of the town.

But this stick was not coming down to the northwest. They were coming down right on top of the town, and each of the men could look down and see the town square and the enormous shape of the nine-hundred-year-old church towering above it. The area was well lit by a building on fire across the square, and the descending troopers could see there was a bucket brigade formed by the townspeople trying to extinguish it.

The Germans were also there, and in the bright light from the fire, the drifting parachutes of the Americans were illuminated. The Frenchmen in the bucket brigade stared upward, and the Germans swung their weapons into action and began firing at the descending shapes.

Private Ken Russell looked around him and then at the crowd below. Russell had just turned seventeen, having been a fraudulent enlistee for the past two years.

"I was just a boy, seventeen, I should have been in high school rather than in a strange country. I should have been going to school. I think my class was graduating that night. Sainte-Mère-Église was the area that we had to take, and as we came in, there was a building on fire. The fire gave light for miles around, and we came in, and when we saw the fire, we jumped. I knew we were in trouble, and it was so horrifying, because most of our stick were killed."

Russell floated down. He had been in the middle of the stick, and already the first men were touching down. But the Germans were waiting for them.

"They didn't even hit the ground," said Russell. "They hit the telephone poles—Lieutenant Cadish, H. T. Bryant, and Laddie Tlapa landed on telephone poles down the street, and it was like they were crucified there. Coming down, one fellow had a Gammon grenade on his hip, and I looked to my right, and I saw the guy, and instantaneously, I looked around and there was just an empty parachute coming down. He was blown away."

Troopers John Blanchard and John Blankenship landed in trees across from the church and the town square. Dead on

DOUGLAS BRINKLEY AND RONALD J. DREZ

landing, Blankenship hung lifelessly in his harness. Blanchard frantically cut through his risers to free himself and drop to the ground. Such was his excitement that he cut off one of his fingers, not realizing it until morning. The rest of the stick floated down into the brightly lit square. One man sailed directly into the fire.

"I finally hit the roof of the church first," said Russell, "and a couple of my suspension lines went around the church steeple and I slid off the roof. I was hanging on the edge of the roof, and John Steele had come down and his chute covered the steeple."

Trooper Steele had no hope of getting down. He was snagged and tangled high up on the belfry, almost fifty feet off the ground. Private Ken Russell was in better shape. He hung at the full extent of his lines, his heels twenty feet from the hard surface of the town square. But he still had to cut himself free and endure the fall. But before he could even try, a German guard saw him.

"I was on the right side of the church, and Steele was hung up on the steeple, and Sergeant [John] Ray came down and missed the edge of the church, but he hit in front of it. A Nazi soldier, billeted on the next street behind the church, came around from behind the church. He was a red-haired German soldier, and he came to shoot Steele and myself, who were still hanging there. As he came around, he shot Ray in the stomach, and John, being a sergeant, had been armed with a .45 pistol, and Ray, while he was dying in agony, got his .45 out and when this German soldier started turning around to us, he shot him in the back of the head and killed him."

Russell freed himself and ran out of town, alone. Gathering his wits, the teenager heard the sound of one of the German flak guns blazing away at the low-flying aircraft and crawled to within grenade distance. He tossed his Gammon grenade in and destroyed the gun. Of his stick of sixteen men who had jumped, only six survived the disastrous drop on the town.

Toward early morning, Private John Fitzgerald of the 101st Airborne found himself alone and extremely thirsty.

"While looking for water to fill my canteen, I spotted a well at the rear of a nearby farmhouse. On my way to the well, the scene I came upon was one that has never left my memory. It was

Private Dwayne Burns stands on the beach with a large collection of equipment.

"ON MY WAY TO THE WELL, THE SCENE I CAME UPON WAS ONE THAT HAS NEVER LEFT MY MEMORY. IT WAS A PICTURE STORY OF THE DEATH OF ONE 82ND AIRBORNE TROOPER. HE LEFT A GRAPHIC HERITAGE FOR ALL TO SEE. HE HAD OCCUPIED A GERMAN FOXHOLE AND MADE IT HIS PERSONAL ALAMO. IN A HALF CIRCLE AROUND THE HOLE LAY THE BODIES OF NINE GERMAN SOLDIERS."
—PRIVATE JOHN FITZGERALD

a picture story of the death of one 82nd Airborne trooper. He left a graphic heritage for all to see. He had occupied a German foxhole and made it his personal Alamo. In a half circle around the hole lay the bodies of nine German soldiers. The body closest to the hole was only three feet away, a potato masher clutched in its fist. The other distorted forms lay where they fell, testimony to the ferocity of the fight. His ammunition bandoliers were still on his shoulders, empty of M-1 clips. Cartridge cases littered the ground. His rifle stock was broken in two, its splinters adding to the debris. He had fought alone, and, like many others that night, he had died alone. I looked at his dog tags. The name read Martin V. Hersh. I wrote the name down in a small prayer book I carried, hoping someday I would meet someone who knew him. I never did."

The parachute regiments were in. The American glider regiments came in on their heels, but experienced terrible casualties—not at the hands of the Germans, but because of the obstacles of the hedgerows that surrounded the small farm fields of the countryside.

"We could hear the sounds of planes in the distance, then no sounds at all," said Fitzgerald. "This was followed by a series of swishing noises. Adding to the swelling crescendo of sounds were the tearing of branches and trees followed by loud crashes and intermittent screams. The gliders were coming in rapidly, one after the other, from all different directions. Many overshot the field and landed in the surrounding woods, while others crashed into nearby farmhouses and stone walls. The gliders had been loaded with heavy guns, radios, and other arms too large to drop by parachute. The cargo was strapped down and secured to plywood floors between the glider troops who had only canvas and light wood to protect them. In a moment, the field was complete chaos. Equipment broke away and catapulted as it hit the ground, plowing up huge mounds of dirt. Bodies and bundles were thrown all along the length of the field. Some of the glider troopers were impaled by the splintering wood of the fragile machines."

Because of terrible dispersion and crashed gliders, the Airborne was fighting in small bands. The unintended conse-

DOUGLAS BRINKLEY AND RONALD J. DREZ

The paratroopers were able to secure the town of Sainte-Mère-Église and the paths leading to Utah Beach. Here Fred Patheiger (driving) and other members of the 101st Airborne are shown after the battle.

quence was the confusion of the Germans as to the size of the fighting force.

Company I of the 505th Regiment of the 82nd Airborne, in one of the most successful drops of the entire airborne force, quickly had over one hundred men on the march to Sainte-Mère-Église.

"When I landed I didn't know where I was," said veteran First Sergeant Howard Melvin. This was his third combat jump, his having jumped in Sicily and Italy. "The people in the group I was in were kind of scattered. People were [huddled] around under ponchos looking at maps and trying to orient themselves. I saw a little farmhouse, and I went over there and knocked on the door. I pointed to my American flag and said, 'Sainte-Mère-Église,' and the Frenchman said, 'That way!'"

Company I took the town just after 4 a.m.

"The town was taken," said Sergeant Bill Tucker, "and the battalion commander should have gotten more credit. He was called 'Blood and Guts Krause'; he was the guy that in England before we left had held up the flag and said, 'This is the flag that flew over Gela in Sicily, and Salerno, and tomorrow morning I will be at the mayor's office and it will be flying over Sainte-Mère-Église,'—and it did fly."

The roads leading to Utah Beach were now blocked to the Germans.

Chapter

6

CROSSING THE CHANNEL: THE AIR AND SEA ARMADAS

The months preceding the invasion had not been idle for the Allied air forces. First, the bombers had been conducting unrelenting air war against German oil assets, and second, more recently, they had shifted their attacks to German rolling stock as demanded by Eisenhower's Transportation Plan.

These massive air attacks did not come without cost. German flak and fighter planes extracted a fearful toll. More than two thousand planes were lost with their crews, and twelve thousand men were killed, wounded, or captured.

These air forces would now shift to a third mission, one to which they were not accustomed. They were now called upon to provide tactical and close air support for the invading army.

The dictates of the Deception Plan precluded massive bombing of the Normandy beaches in the days before the invasion. On June 3, more than half the bombing runs were directed over Calais, and on the following day most of the missions were flown over insignificant targets. The pilots called these "milk runs."

But on D-Day, the air forces were scheduled to fly a staggering fourteen thousand missions, beginning with bombardment of the invasion area and then shifting to areas of possible enemy buildup and targets of opportunity.

 Disk 1, Tracks 22–25: Crossing the Channel by air and by sea

OPPOSITE: Allied invasion ships fire at Luftwaffe planes in the night sky off the Cotentin Peninsula. In the left foreground is a sinking Allied ship.

TIME LINE

JUNE 6, 1944

Dec. 7, 1941	Jan. 15, 1944	June 4, 1944	June 5, 1944	0015–0300	0530
Japan attacks Pearl Harbor; American enlistments increase	Eisenhower becomes supreme commander; planning intensifies	Resistance operatives in France put on D-Day alert	Eisenhower makes decision to proceed with invasion	Airborne troops land in Normandy (British to the east, then Americans to the west)	**Allies bomb beaches; first ground troops land on an island off Utah Beach**

0630	0700	0730–0745	0930–1330	1203	1300	1600	2400
H-Hour on Utah and Omaha Beaches	U.S. Army Rangers scale Pointe du Hoc	H-Hour on Gold, Sword, and Juno Beaches	Troops advance inland	British commandos meet airborne troops at Orne bridges	U.S. 4th Infantry meets 101st Airborne at Pouppeville	Tanks move inland from Omaha Beach	Five beach-heads secured; liberation under way

The 9th Air Force assigned 360 B-26 Marauders like this one to conduct the bombing runs on Utah Beach.

Roger Lovelace was with the 386th Bomb Group and had been training since 1942. He had trained with Jimmy Doolittle to be one of the Tokyo Raiders before a car wreck took him out of that historic mission. Now he trained for a second historic day. He was closing in on his sixtieth mission, far in excess of the original twenty-five needed for rotation back to the States.

During the days leading up to June 6, as Lovelace flew to and from his missions, he could look down at the English countryside and see the massive buildup. Fields were full of the equipment of war. There was hardly one field or one rural road that was not filled with tanks, trucks, and artillery. Boats against the banks were tied off five and six wide.

"By the afternoon of June 5, there were crews painting the black and white invasion stripes on every one of our aircraft. We, as enlisted men, weren't told anything, but we'd just sit there on what seemed like a live bomb with the fuse sizzling, knowing full well that something was going to happen within hours."

Lieutenant Alfred H. Corry flew a B-26 Marauder for the 387th Bomb Group. "I was awakened at 2 a.m. from a sound sleep. The officer of the day came running, shook me, and said, 'Come on, get up, Corry—time to get up.' So we went around and started waking the rest of the guys up. 'We're going to have breakfast in half an hour, then briefing thirty minutes later.'"

The briefing was conducted by one of the command pilots, who had his hat cocked back on his head and a short, stubby cigar in his mouth.

"He said, 'Hey guys, good morning, good morning, good morning! Well, here we are. This is the big day we've been waiting for. That's what we all came here for.' He hadn't said a word yet about a mission, but finally he said, 'We're going to France at 0600 as air support for the Allied forces invading the Normandy coast of Europe.'"

The briefing rooms all over southern England buzzed with excitement as, one by one, the aircrews learned about the invasion and their missions.

Lieutenant John Robinson flew with the 344th Bomb Group. "On March 6, 1944, I had my first combat sortie. The training was over. By the end of May I had flown thirty-one missions."

Robinson felt like an infantryman in World War I—always going over the top of a trench into enemy fire. "We go over the top every day," he said. "We attack and are attacked. We kill and our men get killed every day. It was our job to prepare the ground to the best of our ability to enable the infantry to get ashore, to stay ashore, and fight, and win. We also hoped that while they were about, they'd kill a whole bunch of those damned antiaircraft gunners for whom we had no love and no pity."

On the airfields on June 6, it was dark and a steady rain was falling. Crews climbed aboard and thousands of planes came to life with roaring engines and taxied for takeoff.

The flight plan for the aerial attack was for the B-26 Marauders to go in low, as low as five hundred feet if necessary. The heavier bombers, the B-17s, would go in high at twenty thousand feet. A combination of twelve hundred B-17s and B-24s of the U.S. 8th Air Force would strike the British invasion sector and the area around Omaha Beach, while 360 B-26s from 9th Air Force would strike the defenses of Utah Beach.

The massive air armada faced a critical obstacle to the bombing of the beaches. In any air support mission, the ideal way to bomb, while friendly troops are approaching the battle site, is to conduct the bombing runs parallel to the invading

Lieutenant Alfred H. Corry, who flew a B-26 for the 387th Bomb Group, recalled an abrupt awakening on the morning of June 6.

THE CREW
387 Bomb Gp.
556 sq.
Engl. June '43–July '44

The 556th Squad of the 387th Bomb Group was stationed in England from June 1943 to July 1944. Lieutenant Alfred H. Corry (top right in picture) labeled this picture.

force to eliminate the chance of bombs falling on it. At Normandy this was not possible. The great air train would fly from southern England over the English Channel directly to the French coast, drop their bombs, and fly home.

"Under no circumstances were we to turn around," said Lieutenant William Moriarty of the 387th Bomb Group. "If you had mechanical trouble and could not keep up, drop out of the formation but continue to follow the traffic."

The aircraft would make their approaches directly over the landing craft now churning toward the beaches carrying the first waves. Because of the danger of dropping short bombs on friendly troops, 8th Air Force ordered a delay of several seconds from the bomb-release point. General Eisenhower concurred with this decision.

While that decision was understandable, the results were predictable. The thirteen thousand bombs dropped by 329 B-24s sailed over the Omaha Beach target area and exploded harmlessly in the French countryside, as far as three miles inland.

Flight Officer John Brown of the RAF (Royal Air Force) fared much better. He flew a Typhoon Fighter, a low-wing monoplane equipped with a powerful twenty-four-cylinder, 2200-horse-power engine. The Typhoon carried two five-hundred-pound bombs, was armed with four 20mm cannons, and could conduct strafing and dive-bombing missions.

"On all previous trips across the Channel, we had flown at fifty feet above the water to avoid detection by enemy radar," he said, "but on this day, for the first time, we climbed to eight thousand feet, the height from which we normally started our dive-bombing attack.

"We flew parallel to the Cherbourg peninsula, and as we neared the beachhead, we saw the most memorable sight of the war: a line of most of the leading Allied capital ships, battlewagons, cruisers, and destroyers, lobbing shells onto their shore and inland targets. We proceeded inland, and on a road running from Caen to Bayeux, we spotted eight German tanks.

"We turned on our gun and bomb switches, and our reflector sight which we used to aim our guns and bombs. At the leader's command, we went into echelon starboard formation and followed him down as he peeled off. At four thousand feet, we pressed the button on the throttle, which released the bombs, and pulled out of the dive. We then individually attacked the tanks, firing our cannon at them from all angles."

First Lieutenant J. K. Havener copiloted a B-26 for his attack on gun positions at Utah. His colonel, Ben Witty, had briefed his men that morning that this should be a milk run.

"Split-second precision was to be the key to the success of the operation," said Havener, "and our group was to bomb just twenty-one minutes before the troops were scheduled to hit the beachhead.

"We turned west to the IP [Initial Point (of entry)]. Off to the

First Lieutenant John H. Robinson flew with the 344th Bomb Group.

First Lieutenant J. K. Havener bombed areas near Utah Beach on D-Day as part of the 497th Squadron, 344th Bomb Group. This picture of him was taken in December 1944.

right are the flashes of heavy flak guns firing at us. The German guns have opened up on us, and the light flak of tracers and incendiaries and explosive shells light up the sky. If it wasn't so terrifying, it would look just like a fireworks display, but I'd never before been on the receiving end of the largest Fourth of July celebration of all time."

Havener's B-26 continued on the bomb run as the German antiaircraft fire became murderous.

"A ship in our first box takes a flak hit, does a complete snap roll, but recovers and continues on in formation. Unbelievable! Now we're on the bomb run and another of our ships takes a direct hit, blows up, and goes down. Damn Ben Witty and his 'milk run'!"

Sixty-seven of the 360 aircraft attacking Utah Beach failed to release their bombs. Havener's aircraft was not one of them.

"Our targets were gun positions on the cliffs above the beachhead at the eastern side of the Cherbourg peninsula near Barfleur at Saint Martin-de-Varreville."

"After an eternity we dropped the bombs at 0609 and concentrated on getting the hell out of there on a westward course across the Cherbourg peninsula."

Lieutenant Allen Stephens made his run in against the flak. "We went through the heaviest concentration of antiaircraft fire I had yet seen. Tracers and flak explosions were so thick that it looked impossible to get through without being hit. Especially knowing that for every tracer there were six other rounds. The barrage literally filled the air all around us, and the flak explosions made the air alive with fire."

The air attack at Utah was more successful than the bombardment at Omaha Beach. The B-26s led the way.

Meanwhile, the great sea armada that had so impressed every airman on his way to targets in Normandy churned toward the far shore and the anchorage twenty-two thousand yards offshore.

But where were the German air forces and navy? The Germans, who had long anticipated this day, did not actually know it was at hand. There had been no air reconnaissance during the first five days of June, and naval commanders had decided to cancel patrols and a mine-laying operation scheduled for that night due to bad weather—the very weather the massive Allied fleet now moved through undetected. Incredibly, what was left of the German radar system failed to pick up either the air train or the sea armada.

After having been recalled by Eisenhower's decision to postpone the invasion on June 5, the great sea armada again had rolled out into the sea led by 255 minesweepers that swept ten lanes leading to the five invasion beaches in Normandy. Behind the minesweepers came the slowest vessels in the armada, LCT Flotilla 12—thirty-six LCTs carrying the DD (duplex drive) amphibious tanks to land in the first waves to provide armored support for the infantry.

Lieutenant Dean Rockwell commanded a group of sixteen of the vessels headed for Omaha Beach carrying tanks of the 741st and 743rd Tank Battalions. A second flotilla group of twelve LCTs headed for Utah Beach with tanks of the 70th Battalion. To avoid mix-ups, large, white letters 'O' and 'U' were painted on the respective craft.

"There were literally hundreds of ships, as far as the eye can see, coming together in mankind's greatest assembly of craft for a naval mission of landing a force of military on a heavily guarded enemy shore," said Rockwell.

In the confusion of the hundreds of ships sailing into the English Channel, Rockwell lost one of his craft.

"One of my landing craft was missing—one of my sixteen: the LCT 713. I spent a good part of the forenoon trying to find him and I finally located the LCT 713 with a big 'O' on its conning tower, cruising blithely along where all the other ships had great big 'U's on them. When I came alongside, I told the captain to look around and see where he was. 'Oh', he said." Rockwell guided the wayward craft back to the 'O' group.

"Just looking around after we set sail was the most confusing, extraordinary mélange or mess of ships," said Lieutenant Anthony Duke, the captain of LST 530. "They were all moving in

Lieutenant William J. Moriarty was a B-26 pilot for the 387th Bomb Group.

Soldiers packed into landing craft for the final approach to the beaches.

a sense through a funnel towards that Isle of Wight point. Going along in columns was not an easy task to keep yourself in position. From time to time, we saw some pretty rough collisions.

"We were the second ship in a column of twelve LSTs. I ordered the barrage balloons pulled down and doused and cut loose. They were really beginning to constitute a danger to anybody who got anywhere near those cables. The cables were loosening and snapping in the wind."

LST 530 carried Churchill tanks, jeeps, trucks, and six hundred officers and men of the British Army destined to assault Gold Beach. From the bridge, Duke looked down on the deck and watched the soldiers come up from below and form into small groups. Some played cards while others slept.

This was Duke's first exposure to combat, and the enormity of D-Day impressed him. He intended to call his own men to the deck along with the British soldiers and make the dramatic announcement that the target was Normandy. The British colonel, a veteran of the North African campaign against Rommel's Afrika Korps, sensed Duke's excitement.

"He came up to me and he put his hand on my shoulder," said Duke. "He said, 'Careful, young fellow. Most of my men have seen the worst of desert warfare, and a good many of them were in France and evacuated through Dunkirk. So I'd advise you to go easy, go quick, and don't get dramatic or emotional.'"

Ronald Seaborne was on an LST bound for Gold Beach. He was attached to the British 50th Division as a naval telegrapher, but he was a forward observer and thus served more like a soldier.

"On embarkation I was sent below and told to find a spot to dump my gear, get a meal, and await further orders. The meal, I remember, was a typical army repast, stew and mash followed by steamed pudding and custard. It stays in my mind because it was served up in an indented tray without any accompanying utensils."

Like the other troops, Seaborne searched for anything with which to transfer the food from his tray to his mouth. Fingers were the natural choice, but Seaborne was ingenious. "It is surprising how effective pencils are as chopsticks, even with army stew!"

DOUGLAS BRINKLEY AND RONALD J. DREZ

After dinner, the call went out for "Hands to church." It was voluntary, but it seemed like all attended. It was time to get right with your Maker.

"Every soldier on board seemed to be at the service which was held on the upper boat deck," said Seaborne. "An army chaplain stood behind a table covered by a tablecloth on which stood a small silver cross. As we waited for the service to begin, the wind started to increase in vigor. A sudden gust flipped up the tablecloth, the cross slipped to the deck and broke in two—utter consternation in the congregation. What an omen!"

Sergeant Warren Breniman was on board an LCT off Omaha Beach. He was with the 149th Engineer Combat Battalion (ECB), and as they arrived in the assembly area, most of his men were seasick from the rough seas.

"We encountered a very, very rough English Channel that night. Landing craft, unlike regular boats, do not roll with the ocean tides. They slap up and down. Consequently, I would guess that somewhere in the neighborhood of 98 percent of us became violently seasick during the evening. And, of course, each eruption of seasickness just tended to make it all the worse for everybody else."

Behind the LCTs, the bombardment fleet began to fire on the Normandy coastline. The show was spectacular.

"When we came up from the hold," said Breniman, "the naval bombardment was in full bloom, and it was really quite awe-inspiring to see these great battleships with their 16-inch guns firing at the coastline. Cruisers and destroyers were closer to the beach and also subjecting many of those points to severe naval gunfire.

"That morning, when it was time to leave the ships and boats, I can't think of anything that most of us wanted to do more than to get off of those pitching ships and get our feet on solid ground and get onto the beach."

Seaman First Class Lawrence Orr was the coxswain on LCVP (Landing Craft, Vehicle and Personnel) 33-3 on USS *Bayfield* off of Utah Beach.

"There were thousands of tracer bullets. There was everything happening. We didn't have to worry about taking a bath. There

"WE ENCOUNTERED A VERY, VERY ROUGH ENGLISH CHANNEL THAT NIGHT. LANDING CRAFT, UNLIKE REGULAR BOATS, DO NOT ROLL WITH THE OCEAN TIDES. THEY SLAP UP AND DOWN. CONSEQUENTLY, I WOULD GUESS THAT SOMEWHERE IN THE NEIGHBORHOOD OF 98 PERCENT OF US BECAME VIOLENTLY SEASICK DURING THE EVENING."
—SERGEANT WARREN BRENIMAN

BEHIND THE LCTS, THE BOMBARDMENT FLEET BEGAN TO FIRE ON THE NORMANDY COASTLINE. THE SHOW WAS SPECTACULAR.

were big salvos falling in the water. I think they were charges from those German 88s, and they'd hit the water right beside our barge, and just great fountains of water would go up in the air and come back down. Thank God that I had a good bilge pump."

Lieutenant Cyrus Aydlett stood on deck on *Bayfield.* He was the ship's stores officer, but while at sea and in combat he served as the ship's coding officer.

"At 0130 we saw, for the first time, actual combat between our air forces and German AAs. We were under way and proceeding to anchorage through the mine-swept channel. We'd been at general quarters since 1030. The nervous tension is quite evident among our crew as we proceed nearer the transport anchorage. We have been under way since 0930 this morning and have not encountered any opposition whatsoever."

Aydlett was mesmerized by the spectacular fire show illuminated against the black sky as the air forces and the airborne flew over the fleet.

"Allied bombers are roaring overhead. AA fire can be seen the entire length of this horseshoe-shaped bay which extends for a distance of approximately twenty-five miles—Utah Beach. At times it looked as if a solid sheet of flame covered the entire area, especially when the bombers were making their run. There were varied color flashes from exploding AA shelters all over the area. The din from the roar of planes, bursting bombs, AA fire, and star shells is beyond description.

"An Allied aircraft is hit! Flames are along the entire fuselage, yet it continues on for three or four minutes—enough time for the crew to bail out. The plane suddenly noses down, gaining momentum as it nears the end of its glorious career. Flames are now trailing for several yards. The crash is with deathlike silence, as the din of battle seems to absorb all additional noises. A huge crimson flash rolls skyward.

"Three other planes are destroyed within a period of five or six minutes. One does not get its bombs away before receiving a direct hit. Fingers of fire branch out in all directions as if a thousand rockets had been fired simultaneously. The others meet their death leisurely gliding far out into the

DOUGLAS BRINKLEY AND RONALD J. DREZ

Guns aboard the USS *Nevada* blast away at enemy emplacements, attempting to weaken the defenses for the landing troops.

bay as if seeking a helping hand that could prolong their lives for a few more precious minutes."

While Lieutenant Aydlett watched the bombardment and antiaircraft fire, news of the landings spread fast among the Germans. At 0215, 7th Army placed all defenders on the highest alert. Wire communications in the Corps sector went to all units of the German Army, Navy, and Air Force.

By 0220 German Naval Commander Normandy Walther Hennecke had correctly reported that paratroopers had landed near the Marcouf battery. Reports from the entire sector poured in. Piecing the reports together, Generalmajor Max Pemsel, the 7th Army chief of staff, recognized that the long-anticipated invasion had begun. By 0300 he had judged the main efforts to have targeted Carentan and Caen.

But Pemsel's report was shrugged off by his superiors who thought the attack was a diversion to the main attack, which would come at Pas-de-Calais.

Chapter

7

UTAH BEACH

The massive armada arrived in the Bay of the Seine off the Normandy coast under the cover of darkness. By 0330 the troop transports were disgorging their cargos of soldiers from their tightly packed quarters below deck into small landing craft that rocked and pitched in the three-foot seas.

On one of the transports, *Susan B. Anthony*, the soldiers of the 294th Combat Engineers were out of the war before they could climb down the nets, victims of a German mine.

"We got the order to put our packs on and get ready to disembark," said PFC Archie Sanderson. "I had my pack on and was reaching for my rifle when there was a loud noise. The ship shook all over and all of the lights went out and we were in pitch dark. The ship had struck a mine and started sinking. Lucky for us, it was at the stern of the ship where it struck and not the bow where we were located. Everyone was shouting; we were scared, but there was no panic to run for the stairs. One of the thoughts in my mind was how ironic it would be to die before getting into combat after all of our hard training.

"Our captain calmed the men down and told us to take off our packs and prepare to abandon ship. I placed my rifle on my top bunk so that if I couldn't get out, I had the option of dying by a bullet rather than letting the water close in on me in the pitch dark."

While the men aboard *Susan B. Anthony* abandoned ship, other soldiers of the invasion force descended cargo nets hanging from rails of the troop transports. In groups of four, they climbed down, holding on to the vertical rope strands while their feet sought the horizontal ones.

Disk 2, Tracks 1–4:
Invading Utah Beach

OPPOSITE: A "Force U" LCT carries troops bound for Utah Beach.

TIME LINE	Dec. 7, 1941	Jan. 15, 1944	June 4, 1944	June 5, 1944	JUNE 6, 1944	0015–0300	0530
	Japan attacks Pearl Harbor; American enlistments increase	Eisenhower becomes supreme commander; planning intensifies	Resistance operatives in France put on D-Day alert	Eisenhower makes decision to proceed with invasion		Airborne troops land in Normandy (British to the east, then Americans to the west)	Allies bomb beaches; first ground troops land on an island off Utah Beach

0630	0700	0730–0745	0930–1330	1203	1300	1600	2400
H-Hour on Utah and Omaha Beaches	U.S. Army Rangers scale Pointe du Hoc	H-Hour on Gold, Sword, and Juno Beaches	Troops advance inland	British commandos meet airborne troops at Orne bridges	U.S. 4th Infantry meets 101st Airborne at Pouppeville	Tanks move inland from Omaha Beach	Five beach-heads secured; liberation under way

An Allied general descends into a landing craft for the trip to shore.

"Men in full battle gear had to climb down the cargo nets," said Sergeant John DeVink of Company D, 87th Chemical Mortar Battalion. "Some had their arms or legs smashed as they tried to jump into the landing craft. In addition to my regular battle gear, I had a forty-pound radio and a portable telephone to carry. We were packed like sardines in the landing craft. Mortar carts and all."

Once the craft were loaded, the coxswains of the LCVPs pulled away and circled, waiting for the rest of the craft to rendezvous before they could make their run to the beach.

"We circled endlessly, it seemed, under the huge guns of the battleship *Texas*," said DeVink. "I had never heard or seen a battleship firing a salvo, and, lo and behold, when they did fire, it felt as though our landing craft was lifted clean out of the water, such was the suction as the huge shells traveled overhead."

The battleships *Arkansas* and *Nevada* added their firepower to the beach pounding. When that fire lifted, the men of the United States 4th Infantry Division would be first in at Utah Beach. The men had all studied the terrain models and maps and knew that their landing would be across the beaches and then up four narrow causeways over flooded fields. No one needed to tell them that their columns, restricted to the causeways, would be sitting ducks for an enemy force blocking the roads with automatic weapons. Maneuver in the fields was impossible because the Germans kept them flooded by controlling the locks and the tidal rush of the English Channel. They kept the gates open at high tide to let the water in and then closed the gates on the falling tide to keep the water in the fields. The low land behind the beaches was a quagmire for two miles.

The plan was to land armor in the first wave. British general Percy Hobart had designed a "swimming tank" called a "DD tank" because of its duplex drive that operated propellers off of its main engine. While in the water the tank inflated a waterproof canvas screen. Fully submerged it looked like a small, one-man, canvas dinghy. But when it emerged from the deeper

DOUGLAS BRINKLEY AND RONALD J. DREZ

The battleship *Arkansas* was one of three large gun boats that pounded Utah Beach on D-Day.

water it took on its full dimension and resembled some primordial beast roused from the deep.

These thirty-two DD tanks were carried in eight LCTs and made up Companies A and B of the 70th Tank Battalion. They were to go in first with the assaulting battalions and to proceed inland as fast as they could to link up with the airborne units. Company C consisted of regular tanks under the command of Captain John Ahearn.

"C Company's role was to be in support of Companies A and B, and to also take care of the lateral defenses on the beach."

But before any of the force could cross the line of departure and assault the beach, there was more trouble in the Channel. Four control vessels were to lead the assault waves in, keeping them on line and guiding them on the paths to their respective landing areas.

Utah Beach was divided into Green and Red sectors. Lieutenant Howard Vander Beek commanded LCC 60 (Landing Craft Control 60), the secondary control vessel for Green Beach. He was a veteran of the landings in Sicily.

"PC 1261 and LCC 80, primary and secondary control vessels for Red Beach, were obscured from our view by mist and darkness several yards to our right," he said. "Ahead, on the low, silhouetted beach, we could observe little or no activity. But we knew the enemy was there; they continued to fire at us! But in time we gave their barrage little more than cursory attention.

The pilot of this smoking craft managed to land it safely on shore.

"Then, suddenly, a deafening, thunderous roar sounded behind us, then over us, then ahead of us. *Nevada* led the ships out at sea in a saturating, long-range bombing of the beach defenses. Over us drenching streaks of fire from rocket launchers whooshed to the shore. Tons of destructive force fell upon the mist-shrouded, open-air theater only yards in front of us. Violent explosions and colossal blazes changed the scene, and bursts of smoke, dust, and scurrying sand curtained our view."

During this welcome bombardment, there was some bad news. LCC 80 was tangled up in the assembly area, having fouled one of its screws on a dan buoy that had been placed to guide the landing craft to the beach.

Then, at 0540, more bad news: A German artillery round ripped into PC 1261.

"We saw the PC 1261 suddenly go off course to starboard. Within five minutes, dead in the water, with mainmast down and men going over the side, she sank," said Vander Beek.

DOUGLAS BRINKLEY AND RONALD J. DREZ

Lieutenant Sims Gauthier, senior officer and navigator, watched helplessly. "At seven thousand yards off the beach, I saw PC 1261 just slowly rolling over and the stern went down rather fast. Neither could I nor anyone else stop and pick them up, and this is really a sad part to go through, seeing these men screaming, hollering, and asking for help. So now Red Beach doesn't have any control vessel at all, and that immediately set up a state of confusion."

With no control vessels to lead them in, the LCTs, with their DD tanks, tried to form some sort of a line. But they steamed in all directions, some trying to avoid men in the water.

"It was just like geese flying in the flock when the leader is killed," observed Gauthier.

He went down to the navigator's table to continue to plot the course into Green Sector. He had not been down for five minutes when another explosion threw him from his stool.

"The first thing I knew was that our little craft was lifted up out of the water and we came down again and there was a shock wave that came through that vessel. An LCT with four DD tanks had just been blown sky high and everything disappeared in a matter of seconds."

It was another mine, the victim this time LCT 607, with four tanks and crews, and seventeen naval personnel. Lieutenant Sam Grundfast was commanding.

"A signal was sent to form a line abreast from a column. A few minutes thereafter, when we were almost a line abreast, we hit a mine powerful enough to destroy a ship, let alone a small boat. It literally blew us sky-high. The other officer in the boat was killed. All the men were killed except two men and myself. The four tanks were lost.

"When I opened my eyes, the next thing I knew, I was underwater. I opened my eyes, I looked up, and I saw the surface of water somewhere above my head."

Chaos reigned in the assembly area. With H-Hour just twenty minutes away, the landing was not organized. The captain of PC 1176 summoned Vander Beek and Gauthier over and ordered them to go to ships heading for Red Beach

Lieutenant Sam Grundfast was the captain of LCT 607 on D-Day. He was one of only three survivors when his vessel hit an underwater mine.

Infantrymen aboard an LCI watch as a German mine explodes on the beach off their port bow.

and try to sort things out. He would handle Green Beach as best he could. He made a key decision to try to get the invasion back on schedule so the tanks would arrive on the beach with the infantry.

"Instead of dispersing the tanks into the water at five thousand yards, as planned," said Gauthier, "we would disperse them at three thousand yards. We had begun with thirty-two tanks and lost four, so from three thousand yards from the beach we dispersed the remaining twenty-eight. I went around with the loud-hailer to all the commanders of the DD tanks and gave them instructions that I was going to change my position away from the middle point of Green Beach and assume a new position in this four-hundred-yard lane that separated Red and Green Beaches.

"I gave them instructions that those that were scheduled on Green Beach [were] to stay so many yards on my starboard, and the others on Red Beach to stay so many yards on port; and we led them in that way."

DOUGLAS BRINKLEY AND RONALD J. DREZ

"By 0615, the primary control vessel for Green Beach had dropped a dan buoy at her station to mark the line of departure for the invasion waves," said Lieutenant Howard Vander Beek. "We went to that point to lead in Wave 1, the first of the LCVPs, and Wave 1A, the DD tanks."

Vander Beek had never seen a DD tank before. They seemed almost comical, and he could not take his eyes off them as they struggled to the beach.

"They were odd-shaped sea-monsters depending upon huge, doughnutlike, canvas balloons for flotation, wallowing through heavy waves and struggling to keep in formation as they followed us," he said. "In reality, inside the queer water-wings were thirty-three-ton Sherman tanks."

The landing waves were almost back on schedule, but it seemed that the infantry would land before the tanks. The Germans were shelling the beach and rounds whistled overhead.

"Geysers of sea water were coming from shell fire aimed at us," said Bruce Bradley, a forward observer from the 29th Field Artillery Battalion with the first wave of infantry. "We had to keep our heads down, which made it seem more chilling as to what we would see when the ramp goes down. The noise of the shelling and counterfire was much louder now, and then a deafening blast and we were thrown down or knocked sideways. We had been hit by a shell. The coxswain was gone, the ramp was down, the boat was sinking—sideways. I dog-paddled toward the shore until my feet found sand."

The first wave of infantry continued toward the shore, actually passing the slow-moving DD tanks.

In the first wave was the oldest man in the invasion, Brigadier General Theodore Roosevelt Jr., cousin to the president, and son of former president Theodore Roosevelt. He was fifty-six years old and had a troublesome heart, but had requested to go in the first wave, reasoning that his presence could only boost morale. Major General Barton, the 4th Infantry Division commander, first refused, but then relented.

The boats in the first wave hit the sandbars. Some coxswains gunned their engines, crested the outer bars, and

Sergeant Malvin R. Pike, Company E, 8th Infantry Regiment, 4th Infantry Division, was ashore with the first wave on D-Day.

Troops reaching the sand dunes on Utah Beach stayed low and returned fire.

drove in closer. Sergeant Malvin Pike was in one of the LCVPs with Company E of the 8th Infantry Regiment.

"He got off the bar, and went a hundred feet farther, and he hit another one, and he started again, 'This is it, I can't make it. Y'all gonna have to get out.' Finally, the lieutenant said, 'Pull the pin, drop the ramp.' And the Navy guy couldn't get the pin out of the hole. Finally, one of the guys said, 'To hell with this,' and we just all jumped out over the sides. Where I jumped out, the water was about waist deep.

"But we had about two hundred feet to go and you couldn't run. The only thing you could do is kind of push yourself forward, and we finally made it to the edge of the water."

The soldiers of Company E crossed the two hundred yards of open beach, observing close up the German obstacles. Some were topped with mines, which would have been deadly had the boats come in at high tide. General Roosevelt was already on the beach, walking upright with his cane, ignoring German rounds exploding nearby.

Pike came to a stop. "They had a concrete wall, about four feet high, that we had to go over, then a mound of sand behind the

DOUGLAS BRINKLEY AND RONALD J. DREZ

wall. Nothing looked like the map that we saw back in England. After looking over the beach, General Roosevelt said, 'We have landed in the wrong place, but we will start the war from here.'"

The invasion had come ashore almost two thousand yards south of its scheduled landing site. The loss of the control craft, and the German mines, had contributed to the drift to the left. But Roosevelt was there to provide leadership. He ensured that the invasion did indeed start from there, when it might have bogged down in confusion and indecision.

Second on the beach were the tanks. Not the DD tanks of Companies A and B of the 70th Tank Battalion, but the regular tanks of Company C with Captain Ahearn.

"There had been some problem with the DD tanks," he said, "and we were indeed going to be the first tanks on the beach, or alongside some of the Company B tanks. My tanks did not have this flotation gear, but we had been weatherized, and we were able to get into five or six feet of water."

The British commander had maneuvered his eight LCTs carrying Company C close to the beach and discharged them into water of a suitable depth. The tanks of Company C rolled onto Utah Beach just behind the infantry.

"We then proceeded into the beach," said Ahearn, "and it became evident that the beach area was not the same as had been planned. I was faced with a decision as to what to do at this time, and I saw General Teddy Roosevelt on the beach, and got out of my tank and reported to him, and told him who I was and what my mission was. He told me to go ahead, secure the lateral parts of the beach, both north and south, and to get inland as fast as we could."

The combat engineers arrived with the tanks to clear the beach of obstacles and to blow holes in the massive seawall to allow access to the causeways beyond. Sergeant Al Pikasiewicz arrived with the tanks.

"Our objective was to blow up all the obstacles on the beach which were in front of the roadway and the wall. All of our men ran up and tied all their explosives to the steel obstacles, and as they were tying, I dropped my explosives to

"AFTER LOOKING OVER THE BEACH, GENERAL ROOSEVELT SAID, 'WE HAVE LANDED IN THE WRONG PLACE, BUT WE WILL START THE WAR FROM HERE.'"
—SERGEANT MALVIN PIKE

an assigned man and ran down the beach, unwinding the primer cord."

Each of the engineers attached his charges and timers to the primer cord as Pikasiewicz ran toward the wall signaling the lieutenant that all was ready to blow the obstacles. The lieutenant threw a smoke grenade and yelled, "Fire in the hole." They all huddled against the seawall awaiting the detonation.

But just as the fuse was burning, more boats dropped their ramps and the next wave of soldiers stormed ashore, heading for the obstacles rigged with the charges. The engineers yelled, but that only made the charging soldiers drop to the ground and seek shelter directly behind the obstacles.

"'Look what those men are doing—my God, they're laying in on the explosives!'" shouted Pikasiewicz. "So I left the wall and I ran back and I grabbed some of them by their field packs, yelling, 'Get the hell out of here because this is ready to blow,' and I pulled six men and yelled to the rest. I headed back towards the wall, and when I was fifteen feet from it, it all blew."

Sergeant Richard Cassidy of Company C, 237th ECB was wounded as he came across the beach heading for his objective, the seawall. "Someone came along and took one of my satchel charges, and I lay there and watched them, and they laid seven hundred pounds of explosives on the seawall. It was a hell of a wall. Someone threw a grenade down, yelling, 'Fire in the hole,' and there's guys walking on top of the wall when it went off."

It was still before 0700. German artillery from a huge fortified position to the north at Les-Dunes-de-Varreville was shelling the beach. General Roosevelt sought shelter in one of the shell craters, still scoffing at the need for a helmet as he pulled his knitted woolen hat over his ears. Tanks on the beach and in the surf returned fire toward the German position. Ironically, had the force landed where it was supposed to, the German battery would have been right in the middle of the invasion area.

The invasion at Utah Beach, which had begun with such confusion, immediately progressed into the attack. Already,

Reinforcement troops landing after Utah Beach was secured still faced potential shelling from long-range German guns. Here troops from the 9th Infantry Division stand behind the seawall as others head inland.

the tanks were securing the flanks and the engineers breached eight fifty-yard lanes through the beach obstacles. As they went about their work, the unflappable Roosevelt walked among them.

"General Roosevelt was there, walking up and down the beach with his cane," said the wounded Sergeant Cassidy. "I called out, 'Go knock that bastard down, he's going to get killed.'" But the general simply moved on, inspiring everyone.

By 0830 there was a noticeable slackening of artillery fire on the beach and from then on it was sporadic. Unknown to the soldiers on Utah Beach, the decrease in fire was the result of a

Sergeant Don Malarkey, Company E, 506th Parachute Infantry Regiment, 101st Airborne Division was among the paratroopers who attacked the Germans from behind their lines to open a hole in the defense at Utah Beach.

daring attack by thirteen men from Company E of the 101st Airborne Division just three miles off the beach.

The Germans had placed a battery of four 105mm guns, with a fifty-man crew, in the fields of a farm called Brecourt. Their purpose was to cover Causeway #2 and the exit off the beach. The Germans had been firing since 0630 on pre-planned targets. For two hours the battery hammered away at the beach area, with spotters directing the fire from positions close to the beach.

Suddenly mortar rounds began landing upon the German position and an infantry attack crashed in on their right flank. Thirteen paratroopers engaged the larger German force. The paratroopers had been trying to recover from a scattered drop that landed them in the vicinity of Sainte-Mère-Église when their objective had been Carentan, miles away. Throughout the night the small band, led by Lieutenant Richard Winters, followed narrow farm roads flanked by towering hedgerows, toward its objective.

The plan was to attack on line, with two men providing flanking fire from a concealed position. Sergeant Carwood Lipton and another trooper were assigned to deliver flanking fire.

"When Ranney and I got out to our position to the right, we found that heavy brush and groundcover prevented us from seeing into the gun positions or seeing any of the enemy positions. I heard fire from the front and knew that the men going in on the frontal attack would be needing our flanking fire. So I decided to climb into the trees. There were no large trees with a large single trunk. There were smaller trees and I found that in climbing up into these smaller trees, I had to settle myself down among branches on the front side in order to be able to see in the direction of the enemy.

"It gave me a ringside seat, looking right down into the German positions that were only seventy-five yards away. Then I saw Guarnere and Lieutenant Compton running into the German positions throwing grenades as they went."

"We proceeded towards the first gun," said Sergeant Don Malarkey. "As I neared the gun, I could see the crew of two

DOUGLAS BRINKLEY AND RONALD J. DREZ

Germans firing the 105s straight down the field. I pulled a grenade and threw it, but the two gunmen were already hit by the fire from Buck Compton and [Richard] Winters. When I got there, one was dead lying under the gun, and the other one had run out into a field."

Lipton climbed down from the trees. "When I reached the first gun position, Lieutenant Winters was still there but the breech of the gun was blown out like a half-peeled banana. He said he dropped a block of TNT down the barrel and since TNT requires a percussion cap, Bill Guarnere had dropped a German potato-masher grenade down the barrel with it and that had done it. The other guns were taken one by one."

The small band of Americans had overwhelmed a German force three times its size and knocked out the four guns covering Causeway #2. From then on, the men of the 4th Division moved quickly over the flooded area to link up with the airborne who had successfully blocked any German maneuver to reinforce the beach defenses.

Sergeant Leland Baker of the 101st was on the road leading from the beach. In the distance he saw soldiers approaching.

"I saw a platoon of men coming up the road way down in the distance. I was unsure who they were. They got closer and I could very easily see that four-leaf clover on their left shoulder, which was the insignia of the 4th Infantry Division. Their lieutenant called out to me, he said, 'How're you doing there, paratrooper?' I said, 'Fine, sir, how are you doing?' He said, 'Well, I don't know yet. This thing just started for us.' I said, 'Well, likewise here.'"

With that casual meeting, the seaborne force had linked up with the airborne force. Utah Beach had been a spectacular success not to be imagined from its shaky start. American small-unit leaders had excelled in overcoming the unexpected. They had an excellent leader in General Theodore Roosevelt Jr. For his action on D-Day, he would receive the Medal of Honor. In just one month, on July 12, Roosevelt died of a heart attack.

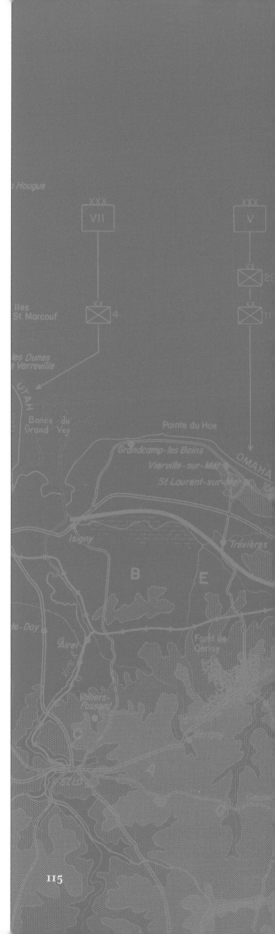

THE RANGERS
AT THE POINTE

In the eighteen-mile gap between Omaha Beach and Utah Beach there was an ominous prominence called Pointe du Hoc. Both Generals Eisenhower and Bradley were very worried about this particular piece of terrain since intelligence had identified six large guns placed on the prominence.

"Pointe du Hoc was equidistant between Omaha and Utah Beaches," said Lieutenant James Eikner, who as a member of the 2nd Ranger Battalion would be part of the attacking force. "The six 155-millimeter guns had a 25,000-yard range and they could rain much destruction down on either of the beaches and reach far out into the sea and cause tremendous damage to naval craft out there. So this installation was to be the most dangerous within the invasion area. Its early neutralization on D-Day morning was considered the primary objective for that day."

"Towards the sea," Eikner continued, "the cliffs dropped off about a hundred feet on the average from vertical to near vertical to actually overhang."

The importance of Pointe du Hoc to the Allied planners is clearly shown by the neutralizing fire they focused on this position. The heavy warships had eighteen targets on

 Disk 2, Tracks 5–11: Capturing Pointe du Hoc

OPPOSITE: A squadron of A-20 "Havoc" bombers return to base after a preparatory raid on Pointe du Hoc, France (April 15, 1944). The huge German gun emplacements at the point (enveloped here in a cloud of smoke) weathered many air attacks to present a formidable obstacle on D-Day.

TIME LINE

Dec. 7, 1941	Jan. 15, 1944	June 4, 1944	June 5, 1944	JUNE 6, 1944	0015–0300	0530
Japan attacks Pearl Harbor; American enlistments increase	Eisenhower becomes supreme commander; planning intensifies	Resistance operatives in France put on D-Day alert	Eisenhower makes decision to proceed with invasion		Airborne troops land in Normandy (British to the east, then Americans to the west)	Allies bomb beaches; first ground troops land on an island off Utah Beach

0630	0700	0730–0745	0930–1330	1203	1300	1600	2400
H-Hour on Utah and Omaha Beaches	**U.S. Army Rangers scale Pointe du Hoc**	H-Hour on Gold, Sword, and Juno Beaches	Troops advance inland	British commandos meet airborne troops at Orne bridges	U.S. 4th Infantry meets 101st Airborne at Pouppeville	Tanks move inland from Omaha Beach	Five beach-heads secured; liberation under way

U.S. Army Rangers pack into a British landing vessel (LCA).

their bombardment list for D-Day morning. Pointe du Hoc was number one. The air support plan for the medium and heavy bombers also had it as the top priority. Failure of the invasion at other places along the sixty-mile front might be overcome, but failure at the point could spell disaster. General Bradley called the task of knocking out the Pointe du Hoc defenses the toughest of any task assigned on D-Day.

To neutralize these guns, Eisenhower had conceived of a daring cliff-climbing attack using grappling hooks fired from special mortars installed on each of the landing craft that would take the attacking force to the Pointe. This attack relied heavily upon surprise. It was reasonable to presume that the German defenders would not expect a force to attempt to scale the hundred-foot sheer cliffs, so that's exactly what Eisenhower planned.

DOUGLAS BRINKLEY AND RONALD J. DREZ

Lieutenant Colonel James Earl Rudder was chosen to lead the force consisting of the 2nd and 5th Ranger Battalions. The plan sounded simple. It wasn't.

Company C of the 2nd Battalion would make an initial, separate attack on a small prominence just to the east of the Pointe called Pointe et Raz de la Percée. This would be an attack that would mostly support the effort at Omaha Beach to help eliminate German flanking fire on the western end. But the main attack, the attack to eliminate the devastating firings of the big 155mm guns, would come at the Pointe itself.

To attack Pointe du Hoc, Companies D, E, and F of the 2nd Battalion would assault the cliffs while Companies A and B and the entire 5th Ranger Battalion marked time offshore awaiting the signal that the Pointe had been taken. If that signal came, then they would follow in trace and land to climb the cliffs.

If the signal did not come from Pointe du Hoc that the position had been secured, then the offshore force would head east to Omaha Beach, land there, and move inland to take the Pointe from the rear, advancing along the coastal road.

As the great armada sailed toward Normandy on the night of June 5 and into the early hours of June 6, there was much talk and speculation taking place belowdecks by the men of the Ranger landing force. Some of it was cocky, and some of it was whispered concerns, but most talk exuded confidence borne of discipline and training.

Donald Scribner from Company C was belowdeck on the British ship HMS *Prince Charles*. Company C's attack on Pointe et Raz de la Percée would be isolated from the rest of the force.

"I remember quite well going across the English Channel," he said. "It was very rough. The waves were very high. We were about ten miles from shore when Colonel Rudder came down and talked to us prior to loading up the LCAs [Landing Craft, Assault]. He had this comment to make to us. 'Boys, you are going on the beach as the first Rangers in this combat in this battalion to set foot on French soil, but don't worry about being alone. When D, E, and F take care of Pointe du Hoc, we will come down and give you a hand with your objective. Good luck and may God be with you.'"

Captain James W. "Ike" Eikner, 2nd Ranger Battalion, at home in October 1945.

ABOVE: Donald L. Scribner, 2nd Ranger Battalion, Company C. **OPPOSITE:** U.S. Army Rangers scale the rocks at Pointe du Hoc. This picture was taken after the area had been secured.

Company E's Salva Maimone remembers his shipboard experience. "On the boat, we had a little conference with the officers telling us how dangerous this mission was and we were facing great odds. The way they put it to you, . . . with the odds you had there, it was as if you were ready to go to an electric chair, because you didn't have any chance. And it had you feeling tight all the time you were on the boat, and to try to forget about it—we played cards and tried to forget everything. But it went on, and [men] were laughing and carrying on, and the officers said everyone that even gets close to the cliff ought to get an award."

At 0300 on June 6, 1944, the Rangers of Company C were the first to disembark from HMS *Prince Charles*. British sailors stationed themselves to help the Rangers into the assault landing craft that were hanging and swaying in the davits. Unlike the Higgins boats, which were first lowered into the water and then loaded, the British LCAs were loaded with the soldiers before the boats were lowered into the water.

"Down went the landing craft in the davits," said Lieutenant Sidney Salomon, one of the platoon commanders. "All conversation had come to a halt as if everyone had suddenly become mute. All were tense. Now a loud smack as the bottom of the landing craft hit the water. The first landing craft away from the transport began to circle, waiting for the second craft to maneuver into position. When both were in their assigned positions, the parallel trip in the direction of the shore began. We were two small bobbing objects in the choppy waters of the Channel.

"Suddenly there were splashes around the craft, and white, cascading water. Then concentric circles, as shells landed in the water in the vicinity of the landing craft. Sharp pings of bullets against the steel hull sounded, as the defending Germans fired their automatic weapons directly at the landing craft." The Rangers crouched low in the boat, and the coxswain pushed the throttle forward, but the pings on the hull continued.

"I called out the words, 'Get ready', which were passed along to those in the stern of the craft, and everyone inched forward just a little bit.

DOUGLAS BRINKLEY AND RONALD J. DREZ

First Lieutenant Sidney A. Salomon, who commanded the 2nd Platoon of Company C on D-Day and later assumed command of Company B.

"The moment the ramp had dropped down, automatic weapons and rifle fire sprayed the debarking Rangers, killing and wounding several men. The second man was hit by a bullet from a German entrenched at the top of the cliff. I reached over and pulled him clear of the craft, just before the heavy steel-hulled craft would have steamrollered him.

"The Rangers waded to the shoreline and started across the sand, striving to reach the cover of the base of the cliff. Machine-gun, small-arms fire, and mortars cut down some of the men as they attempted to run across the sand."

Quickly the men gathered at the base of the cliff and returned fire to the unseen Germans above. Captain Ralph Goranson, the company commander, ordered the Rangers up the ropes.

"Lieutenant Moody, along with Sergeant Julius Belcher of Schwartz Creek, Virginia, and Otto Stevens of Newcastle, Indiana, scaled the cliffs. These three men free-climbed about a ninety-foot cliff that was partially an incline and then straight up the last fifteen or twenty feet. We gave them covering fire from down below to keep the Germans off their back. The last ten or fifteen feet they chinned themselves up with their trench knives and secured a series of toggle ropes from the barbed wire emplacement up there so the rest of us could immediately move over into this position and climb up the cliff and get into the area around the fortified house.

"Lieutenant Moody, immediately when he got topside, killed the officer in charge of the Germans in the fortified house. We found the rest of the area honeycombed with dugouts, trench systems. And immediately Lieutenant Moody and his men dispatched teams to go and clear up this area; they were followed immediately by the 2nd Platoon with Lieutenant Salomon, and it was right here that we lost Lieutenant Moody. He was downed by a sniper."

That left Lieutenant Salomon to lead the forces on the cliffs. He ordered Rangers in groups of twos and threes to clean out the trenches and holes. Finally the Rangers surrounded the fortified house at the top of the cliff that was the fire direction center of the whole position.

DOUGLAS BRINKLEY AND RONALD J. DREZ

"This was put out of action by Sergeant Belcher who threw in a white phosphorous grenade," said Captain Goranson, "and when the Germans came out, they were sent to heaven by Sergeant Belcher's gun."

"Ultimately, I made it to the top," said Salomon, "and spotted a series of trenches some twenty-five yards distant. I pointed, indicating all should run to the trench. We all ran and leaped in the trench fully prepared to take sole possession, and opposition from the foe soon ended, and I looked around to see who was still with me. Nine men remained from the thirty-nine that had been jammed in the landing craft."

While Company C attacked Pointe et Raz de la Percée, the small flotilla of ten LCAs with Companies D, E, and F headed for Pointe du Hoc. For these companies, things went wrong from the start. One of the supply boats was almost immediately swamped, and sank. The remaining nine pushed on through the rough seas, but while still eight miles off the Normandy coast, a second boat started to fall behind.

Water poured in from the sides and despite a frantic bailing attempt by the Rangers on board, the boat filled with water, faltered, and sank, eliminating one-third of the sixty-five-man force of Company D, including the company commander. Now eight boats, with 225 Rangers, pushed for Pointe du Hoc.

The small force's troubles were not over. As they approached the coast, Colonel Rudder noticed that the prominence to which they were headed was not Pointe du Hoc, but Pointe et Raz de la Percée. He quickly had the helmsmen change course to head parallel to the coast, running a gauntlet of German fire. The other boats followed in a line, two hundred yards off shore.

James Eikner described the predicament. "I can remember when the first small arms hit our boat and it made a noise and somebody said what it was. I looked and there was a little round hole through one of the rope boxes and I said, 'My God these guys are playing for keeps,' and so we all got down. We had been standing up except for those who were bailing water, so we all ducked down. The Germans were taking us under fire like shooting ducks in a tub and it got worse as we got closer to the Pointe."

Captain Ralph E. Goranson, company commander of Company C, born July 4, 1919, in Chicago, Illinois.

After the smoke cleared at Pointe du Hoc, evidence of the Allied bombardment was obvious in the craters left on the beach.

The error in navigation caused a forty-minute delay in getting to the Pointe. The narrow window to signal for the offshore force to follow was almost closed. The rest of 2nd Battalion and all of 5th Battalion would have to be signaled that the Pointe had not been taken and that they were to proceed to Omaha Beach.

The plan had been for Companies E and F to land on the left side of the Pointe while Company D landed to the right, but the delay in the approach changed this. First Sergeant Len Lomell saw an opening between the boats of E and F and ran the remaining two boats of Company D into the narrow gravel beach.

The eight landing craft had a total of forty-eight mortar tubes to fire the grapnels at the top of the cliff. As each boat came ashore, it fired its six grapnels. But of the forty-eight ropes, only twenty-two made it to the top. Still, it was enough. The Rangers began the climb to the top under the fire of the Germans who lobbed grenades down and tried to cut the ropes.

As the Rangers worked their way up hand-over-hand, one of the special amphibious vehicles idled in the choppy water and

DOUGLAS BRINKLEY AND RONALD J. DREZ

raised a unique weapon to dominate the cliffs. Four DUKWs (pronounced "ducks") had been equipped with extension ladders from the London Fire Brigade. One had sunk on the run in and two of the others could not get positioned on the narrow beach. But the fourth edged forward and now lifted its ladder vertically and inched it toward the sky.

On top of the ladder was Staff Sergeant William Stivison, bobbing and weaving with the pitch and roll of the craft while manning the twin Lewis machine guns mounted on the top. As he came even with the level of the plateau, ninety feet in the air, he blazed away while the ladder pitched and swayed like a pendulum. Stivison raked the top of Pointe du Hoc much like a runaway fire hose and tried to aim the unsteady guns at the Germans diving for cover.

The Germans fired back, but had an equally difficult time hitting the elusive sergeant as he swayed back and forth like a target in a shooting gallery. Enemy tracers licked past Stivison, but none found their target. The aerial firefight lasted for a couple of minutes. In the end, the rough Channel won out and Stivison had to be lowered, neither he nor the Germans any the worse for wear.

Now Company D, having abandoned the right side, added the weight of their attack to the left side of the Pointe. Sergeant Lomell was wounded through the side as he stepped from the boat, but continued on and climbed the cliffs. Once up there he gathered his men and rushed forward.

Moving like rabbits running from hole to hole, the small Ranger force advanced toward the three casemated gun positions on the right side of the position where they were originally to have ascended the cliffs.

When they got to the positions, instead of having to attack heavily defended gun emplacements, the Rangers stared into empty pits and casemates.

"And so there were no guns in the positions," said Lomell. "So, we decided, 'Well, they must have an alternate position somewhere.' And we thought, 'We'll hear them. Maybe we'll see some evidence of the movement.' But we never did hear them."

Sergeant Leonard G. Lomell, of Company D, was wounded immediately after stepping from his boat, but continued on up the cliffs in pursuit of the German guns.

The Germans were well fortified at Pointe du Hoc because of the natural cliff barriers and the inset emplacements.

Lomell did not waste time lamenting the empty casemates. Since his primary mission to destroy the guns was not attainable, he immediately turned to his secondary mission, which was to interdict the coastal road that ran behind the Pointe and joined the German positions all the way from Grandcamp to the Sword Beach at Ouistreham.

"We never stopped," said Lomell. "We kept firing and charging all the way through their buildings area, where they came out of their billets in all states of undress. We were confronted with them there on our way up the road from the point to the coast road. Our orders were to set up a roadblock and keep the Germans from going to Omaha Beach. We were to also destroy all communications visible along the coast road."

Lomell's small force from Company D was the first to reach the coastal road, where they set up roadblocks both left and right, but were hardly in position when the sound of marching boots was heard. Quickly, the small Ranger force ducked for cover and a forty- to fifty-man German patrol soon appeared heading in the direction of Utah Beach. Since the force was not heading to Omaha, the outnumbered Rangers let them pass. The Germans turned into a field and faded from sight and the Rangers reset the roadblock.

Lomell and Sergeant Jack Kuhn walked a short distance along the coast road to the right of the intersection, and found a small sunken road that had signs that heavy equipment or wagons had passed. Lomell remembers:

"And so Jack and I went down this sunken road not knowing where the hell it was going, but it was going inland . . . and we came upon this vale, or this little draw, with camouflage all over it, and low and behold, I peeked over this—just pure luck—over this hedgerow and there were the guns, all sitting in proper firing condition, the ammunition piled up neatly, everything at the ready, but they were pointed at Utah Beach. They weren't pointed at Omaha Beach."

Sergeant Lomell lay in the hedges for several moments looking at the abandoned guns. Finally he saw a group of one hundred soldiers in the far corner of the field looking as if they were having a meeting. He saw his chance.

DOUGLAS BRINKLEY AND RONALD J. DREZ

"I said, 'Jack, you cover me, I'm going in there and destroy them.' So, all I had was two thermite grenades. I went in, he covered me. I said, 'Keep your eyes on these people. I won't know if anybody comes, and you keep your eyes open.'"

Lomell crept from his position in the hedgerow and slipped into the field keeping an eye on the German force one hundred yards away. He put one of his two thermite grenades into the elevating and traversing mechanisms of the gun closest to him, and then crawled to the second one and repeated the process.

He pulled the pins and crept back to the hedgerow as the grenades silently ignited. The white-hot heat soon melted the metal of the mechanisms and rendered the guns immovable. They could still be fired, but only in their locked positions. The Germans never turned or moved from their position in the far corner of the field.

"But then we ran back to the road," said Lomell, "which was a hundred yards or so back, and got all the other thermite grenades from the remainder of our guys. I had a dozen guys out there manning a roadblock. So we stuffed them in our jackets and we rushed back, and we put the thermite grenades, as many as we could, in traversing mechanisms and elevation mechanisms and banged the sites."

Lomell again left the field to join Jack Kuhn who was diligently watching the approaches, and the two Rangers started to run away. But a gigantic explosion dropped them both to their faces. Thinking it was a short round from one of the battleships, they scrambled to their feet and ran back to the road. Later they would learn that it had been the destruction of an ammo dump by another Ranger patrol.

With the actions of Sergeants Lomell and Kuhn, the dreaded guns of Pointe du Hoc were neutralized. The cliffs had been scaled, the road between Omaha and Utah Beaches had been interdicted, and the guns had been put out of action. The Rangers had become the first American unit to achieve its D-Day objectives.

For their actions, Lomell received the Distinguished Service Cross and Kuhn was awarded the Silver Star.

Sidney Salomon (who became a captain) received the Silver Star for his bravery at Pointe Du Hoc.

THE 16TH REGIMENT AT OMAHA BEACH

Eighteen-year-old Private Franz Gockel of the 3rd Kompanie, Infanterie Regiment 726 was positioned at *Widerstandsnest* 62 as part of the German defense along the beach between Colleville-sur-Mer and Vierville-sur-Mer. From the German lines he witnessed the events leading up to and taking place on June 6, 1944.

"In February 1944, during his inspection of the defenses of the Normandy coast, Field Marshal Rommel had visited our position," said Gockel. "He had sharply criticized not only the lack of defenses constructed at our position but also those along the entire coastline from Colleville-sur-Mer to Vierville-sur-Mer. He compared the bay in our sector with the bay at Salerno in Italy, and urgently ordered further defenses to be constructed."

Rommel ordered the construction of the massive concrete defensive positions called *Widerstandsnests* and, by June, the German defense bristled with fifteen of these strong points positioned to deliver enfilading fire along the long axis of Omaha Beach, converting it into a formidable killing zone. Since the apertures of the steel-reinforced, concrete positions faced away from the sea, they were virtually invisible, and their six-foot-thick walls and overheads made them impervious to naval gunfire.

 Disk 2, Tracks 12–17: The 16th Infantry at Omaha Beach

OPPOSITE: The invading force at Omaha Beach often had a long way to wade from the landing craft to the shore.

TIME LINE

Dec. 7, 1941	**Jan. 15, 1944**	**June 4, 1944**	**June 5, 1944**	**JUNE 6, 1944**	**0015–0300**	**0530**
Japan attacks Pearl Harbor; American enlistments increase	Eisenhower becomes supreme commander; planning intensifies	Resistance operatives in France put on D-Day alert	Eisenhower makes decision to proceed with invasion		Airborne troops land in Normandy (British to the east, then Americans to the west)	Allies bomb beaches; first ground troops land on an island off Utah Beach

0630	0700	0730–0745	0930–1330	1203	1300	1600	2400
H-Hour on Utah and Omaha Beaches	U.S. Army Rangers scale Pointe du Hoc	H-Hour on Gold, Sword, and Juno Beaches	Troops advance inland	British commandos meet airborne troops at Orne bridges	U.S. 4th Infantry meets 101st Airborne at Pouppeville	Tanks move inland from Omaha Beach	Five beach-heads secured; liberation under way

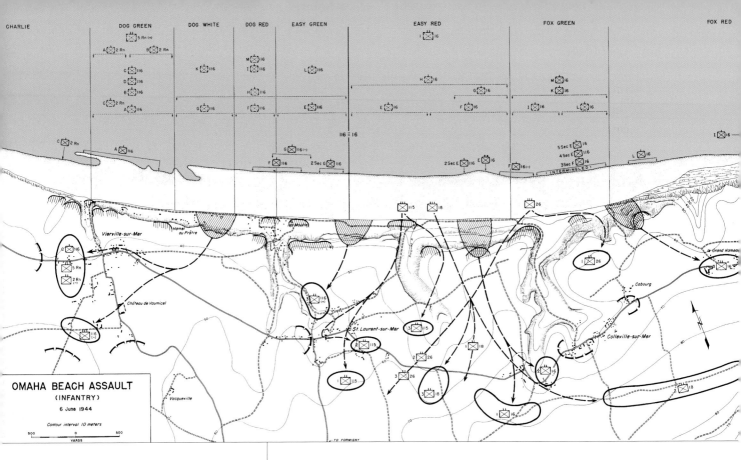

A map of the Omaha Beach invasion area, showing sectors targeted by both the 16th Regiment (to the east) and the 116th (to the west).

"During the several weeks preceding June 6, two casemates for 75mm guns were poured and only the steel aperture covers were lacking," said Gockel. "We constructed tank barriers on the beach at low tide from logs topped with Teller mines. Other beach obstacles were Czech hedgehogs made from crossed iron beams, and Belgian Gates, from thick steel stakes.

"Running parallel to the waterline before us was a low wall made of water-worn stones enclosing the beach, and along the wall was laid a minefield for the purpose of protecting us from surprise attack during darkness. A tank trench had been dug between WN 62 and WN 61 and was protected with mines, and our position was protected with a tangle ring of barbed wire rolls."

Now Gockel and his twenty comrades at WN 62 stood at alert, having been called to quarters at 0200.

"The alarm call into the bunker woke us from a deep sleep," he said. "A comrade stood in the entrance and continued to shout the alarm, to dispel any doubt, and urged us to hurry. We had so often been shaken to our feet by this call in the past weeks that we no longer took the alarms seriously, and some of the men rolled over in their bunks and attempted to sleep. An NCO appeared in the entrance way behind our comrade and brought us to our feet with the words, 'Guys, this time it's for real. They're coming!'"

There had been the reports of parachute landings. But thus far Gockel's sector had remained quiet as he stood straining his eyes toward the sea and shivering in his thin summer uniform. Aircraft flew over and the rumble of bombs could be heard in the distance. Suddenly it seemed that there was movement in the Channel.

"Dark shadows could be detected on the horizon," said Gockel, "and we first believed them to be German patrol craft. But soon the shadows grew and became so numerous that all hope was dispelled. The detectable wake from large and small ships increased in number."

And then as the gray dawn began, Gockel and his comrades saw the great armada.

"An endless fleet lay before our sector. Heavy warships cruised along as if passing in review. A spectacular but terrifying experience."

The LCVPs made their run-in to the beach as the German soldiers watched. The naval gunfire kept many of them pinned down, but the German plan was to hold their fire until the invasion was ashore. Some long-range artillery could fire to sea, but the guns of the beach defenses were oriented to cover the beach.

Al Littke of the 299th ECB was mesmerized by the tremendous firepower demonstrated by the Navy with its big-gun bombardment and its [LCT(R)] rocket ships.

"With all this firepower, it should be a cinch," he said. "I thought I was untouchable. As we were going in, the navy men were using the .50-caliber machine guns, firing over our heads towards the beaches.

"Once I hit the beach, I advanced fifteen feet and lay down. On my left I could see GIs advancing, and I tried to run, and dropped my charges at the steel obstacles and continued up to the break wall, which was like an embankment of stones.

German Private Franz Gockel was eighteen years old at the time of the D-Day invasion. He was part of 3rd Kompanie, Infanterie Regiment 726, stationed at Omaha Beach.

At the Easy Red sector of Omaha Beach, as at other sectors, American infantrymen of Company E, 16th Infantry Regiment, were pinned down and took cover behind anything that was available.

There was plenty of room to lie down behind it, and we were well protected."

The men in the first wave sought shelter behind this low embankment, or "shingle," of loose stones. It defined the high-water mark of the beach and provided the only cover to give a small amount of protection from direct fire.

The beach was zinging with bullets. Often a man's first realization that he was under tremendous fire was to watch another man go down.

"I saw a bunch of GIs lying face down and not moving," said Littke, "and then noticed a GI running up, and all of a sudden he dropped his rifle and with both hands he clutched for his throat and went down. Another man running practically in his footsteps went down and his helmet rolled off."

The German defenses smashed the first wave. Up and down the beach, the carefully planned defensive line unleashed its massive firepower.

DOUGLAS BRINKLEY AND RONALD J. DREZ

"Assault boats and landing craft rapidly approached the beach," said Gockel of WN 62, "and the first closely packed landing troops sprang from their boats, some in knee-deep water, others up to their chests. There was a race over the open beach toward the low stone wall running parallel to the water-line, which offered the only protection. "Now we sprang into action. Now, the first machine gun bursts, and within seconds the first assault wave troops collapsed after making only a few meters headway. I had opened fire with my heavy machine gun with short bursts aimed at the landing boats. A comrade fired round after round from his 75mm gun."

Corporal Robert Miller, 149th ECB arrived at Easy Red sector and watched a jeep roll off the front of his LCT. It disappeared underwater and reappeared, unscathed because it had been waterproofed. Its extended exhaust pipe stuck up like a periscope above the water. The trucks disembarked next, and then the men.

"We dropped completely under with the weight of all our gear," said Miller. "I was able to eject all my equipment with the exception of gas mask and steel helmet, and leap upward from the ocean floor, finally getting my head above water, and started swimming to the beach. The weight of the soaked clothes, boots, gas mask, and steel helmet made it near impossible, but I did reach water hip-deep finally and attempted to stand up. I was near exhaustion by this time and felt as though my body weighed at least three hundred pounds."

Miller waded in, staggering like a drunkard. Hearing screams from behind him, he turned to see men disappear below the surface, pulled down by their water-soaked gear and not able to free themselves.

"I saw ahead of me GIs huddled behind a shale ridge for protection. At last I reached shore and was about fifteen feet up the beach when a big white flash of nothingness enveloped me. I had been hit, and the next thing I knew, I was flat on my back looking up at the sky. I tried to get up but could not, and reasoned, my God, my legs had been blown off since I had no sensation of movement in them."

Robert H. Miller, of the 149th Combat Engineers, was one of those wading to shore at Easy Red Sector of Omaha Beach. He made landfall, but was hit soon after by a bullet to the spine that left him paralyzed.

Sergeant Jerry W. Eades was chief of a section that fired a bow-mounted howitzer as his landing craft came in to shore.

Miller discovered his legs were intact, but a bullet had severed his spine. He took his last steps on Omaha Beach.

The swimming DD tanks, designed to land first and provide the infantry with armored support, were nowhere to be seen when the first men came ashore. Most had been launched far out in the Channel, and had sunk. Only five made it to the beach.

Lieutenant Dean Rockwell, commanding LCT 535, brought his craft to the beach and discharged two tanks directly. He caught the attention of every German gunner.

"As soon as we landed our tanks, we began getting the hell out of there," he said, "but we noticed that some of the tanks were already in trouble. A German 88 in a pillbox, on the extreme right flank of our landing area, protected by heavy concrete overhead and side shields, was firing through a slit and enfilading the entire beach. Initially it concentrated on the LCTs. Two were immediately hit. Three sailors were killed and three wounded on LCT 713. The German 88 turned its attention to the tanks and I could see some of the tanks begin to burn from the direct hits."

The 58th and 62nd Armored Field Artillery Battalions came in eighteen LCTs, each with two 105mm self-propelled howitzers in the bow. Sergeant Jerry Eades was section chief, B Battery, 62nd Battalion.

"Our boat had the #3 and #4 guns, and we knew what our job was and what we were prepared to do, and that was to start firing at approximately eleven thousand yards out, or when our guns came in range of the beach. The officer-in-charge would time the distance we would cover on his watch. He had a small washtub hanging on a string, and a large wooden paddle, and each time the boat would go so many yards by his watch, he would rap this tub like a gong and we would fire one round. The gunner would then immediately change his settings to lower the range fifty yards and reload the gun."

Fifty yards later, the 105s fired again. This continued to within two thousand yards of the beach, where the gunners could not depress the barrels lower.

DOUGLAS BRINKLEY AND RONALD J. DREZ

German gun emplacements similar to this one kept the Allied forces pinned down wherever they could find cover on the beach.

The boats turned, and as they did, German fire smacked the sides of the LCTs. They followed the infantry in, but could not land.

"As we came back in," said Eades, "everything was bogged down on the beach, and the boats slowed to almost a standstill, and we stood by for a possible fire mission."

But no fire mission came. The infantry was pinned down in the German killing zone. Later the LCTs again came in close to unload. But as the guns rolled off the ramps, they went straight to the bottom.

"On came the second wave," said Franz Gockel of WN 62, "and again the race across the beach, and again the defensive fires. More and more comrades were killed or wounded. The tide came slowly forward and the waterline crept up on the beach."

The soldiers landing on Easy Red sector of Omaha Beach usually sought cover behind the steel obstacles on the beach. As the water crept forward with the onrushing tide, they were forced to move. Every man came to the same conclusion. The only safety lay in getting across the beach to that stone embankment.

Soon the embankment was packed with soldiers trying to press against it for safety. As more and more huddled together, the Germans recognized the target.

"The safety offered the attackers was only temporary," said Gockel, "for our mortars lay deadly fire upon preset coordinates

General Rommel had telephone poles topped with mines installed to explode the hulls of invading craft.

along the wall. Mortar rounds with impact fuses exploded on target. The shell splinters, wall fragments, and stones inflicted casualties upon the troops.

"Hour after hour, boats and landing craft assaulted the beach, attempting to gain ground. The wave of attackers broke against our defenses, and as the tide continued to rise, the surf brought a gruesome cargo ashore. In the swells wounded soldiers fought for their lives, and the dead floated and tossed in the water, the waves dumping them onto shore."

Everett Schultheis was in an LCT with a half-track of the 467th Anti-Aircraft Artillery (AAA) Battalion. As he made his run to the beach, he saw the DD tanks struggling to the shore.

"I counted sixteen at one time," he said, "but one by one the screening devices collapsed and the tanks were swamped. Out of sixteen, only two made it ashore, and within seconds, they were knocked out by hostile fire."

The second of the 467th AAA boats came ashore. "We went in, dropped our ramp," said Samuel Reali, "and the Germans hit it, knocking half of it off, and then hit us again, right in the center."

Reali's crippled LCT backed off, bringing its terribly wounded men out to another vessel. But it was not out of the fight yet.

"Then we returned back to the shoreline again and dropped our ramp. We were beginning to sink, but we hit a pier—a cement pier that the Germans had there.

"We dropped the ramp and Lieutenant Dewey jumped off. I never saw him again. We drove off with our half-tracks, which were waterproofed, but the water was so deep that the intake pipes weren't long enough and I went thirty-five feet and the half-track conked out."

Reali took his place on Omaha Beach with hundreds of other men whose smashed vehicles littered the sand. He found another destroyed half-track and dived under.

"Germans started zeroing in and they put three shots around me. Then a soldier, a friend of mine, W. K. Brown, came along and slid right in alongside of me. The fourth shot went off from the German guns, and it splattered him in the side with shrapnel."

Reali dragged Brown away from the vehicle as the Germans continued to pound it. He gave him morphine, shouted for a medic, and pushed on across the devastated beach, attempting to reach the inviting stone wall. Along the way, he stumbled across another comrade.

"I found my friend from A Battery, Sam Depollo, who had gotten shot in the stomach by something that had separated his body into two separate parts—his bottom part was about twenty feet from the top part."

Steve Kellman of Company L landed in knee-high water. He made it past the embankment by ten feet, but still the German mortars found him. "Suddenly shells landed about ten yards away and the concussion flipped me over on my back. A man immediately to my right was killed and I had a numb feeling in my right leg."

Stripping off his leggings, Kellman bandaged his own wound, but could not walk. All he could do was turn around and watch the next boats come ashore.

"HOUR AFTER HOUR, BOATS AND LANDING CRAFT ASSAULTED THE BEACH, ATTEMPTING TO GAIN GROUND. THE WAVE OF ATTACKERS BROKE AGAINST OUR DEFENSES, AND AS THE TIDE CONTINUED TO RISE, THE SURF BROUGHT A GRUESOME CARGO ASHORE. IN THE SWELLS WOUNDED SOLDIERS FOUGHT FOR THEIR LIVES, AND THE DEAD FLOATED AND TOSSED IN THE WATER, THE WAVES DUMPING THEM ONTO SHORE."
—GERMAN PRIVATE FRANZ GOCKEL

Troops of the 16th Infantry Regiment are shown here resting by a chalk cliff that offered temporary protection while they invaded.

"Succeeding waves of ships came in and a great many of the men were cut down coming across the beach. Of a hundred and eighty men in our assault group, only seventy-nine of us came across the beach alive."

Albert Mominee of Company I came in on an LCI with thirty-five men. His boat was two hours late and the water had covered the German-placed obstacles.

"About four hundred yards from shore, the craft gave a sudden lurch as it hit an obstacle and in an instant an explosion erupted, followed by a blinding flash of fire. The LCI was enveloped in flames. Flames raced around and over us. The craft slowly sank, and then stopped, coming to rest on an obstacle buried on the sandy bottom which prevented us from sinking any further."

The soldiers scrambled off the stricken vessel. Those with eighty-pound flamethrowers strapped on never had a chance. In the water they drew the German fire.

"The Germans who were inside of a bunker on top of the cliff overlooking the beach directed machine-gun fire toward the men in the water and toward those men who hadn't left the craft but still clung to it. Only six out of thirty-five escaped unharmed."

"I could see the Germans on top of the bluff about seventy feet up," said PFC Theodore Aufort, "and they were shooting down on us. A large landing craft came and discharged a tank, and I said, 'Thank God for support.'

DOUGLAS BRINKLEY AND RONALD J. DREZ

"He made it through the obstacles, got halfway across the rocks and cobblestones and just sank down, its treads acting like a shovel, and it sank on its belly and couldn't move. But those guys that were inside that thing were letting everything go. They had two machine guns, and they were firing over our heads at the bluffs."

The German fire was merciless. Herbert Campbell's visit to Easy Red sector lasted only a few minutes. He was with the 5th Engineering Special Brigade.

"A German shell hit our landing craft and killed a sailor that was three feet from me, and a man that started down the ramp ahead of me had his arm almost completely severed from his body.

"I got hit in the legs and on the left and right side of my body as I ran onto the beach, and [the] supply sergeant ran past us and yelled, 'Men, let's get off of here or we'll all be killed.'" The medics ran to Campbell within minutes and evacuated him on the same boat.

Omaha Beach was utter chaos. The men huddled, leaderless, in small groups, realizing that large groups attracted German fire. Tanks and vehicles burned, and the plan was a shambles. The idea of a quick landing with troops forming on the beach and exiting up the several draws proved to be fantasy. Bodies and body parts littered the beach, and lifeless corpses tossed and rolled in the surf.

To stay on the beach was suicidal. Each man, in his own time, eyed the dominating high ground, and concluded that the only way off was up the cliffs.

Captain Joe Dawson of Company G had jumped off his landing craft with the first three men, only to see the rest of his boat team perish from a direct hit. Working his way to the shingle, he was joined by nearby survivors of his company.

"A minefield lay in and around a path extending to my right and upward to the crest of the bluff overlooking the beach," said Dawson. "Upon blowing a gap in the concertina wire, I led my men gingerly over the body of a soldier who had stepped on a mine in seeking to clear the path."

Dawson then led two other men up the tiny path where they ran into some other soldiers led by Lieutenant John Spaulding

Steve Kellman, Company L, 16th Regiment, 1st Division, was wounded in the leg on his way up the beach, and, unable to walk, could only lie and watch the successive waves of men coming ashore and being cut down by the German guns.

Sergeant Hyman Haas was part of the 467th Anti-Aircraft Artillery Battalion that turned its guns on the German pillboxes and eventually broke a hole in the German defense.

from Company E. With Spaulding's men covering, Dawson's small team advanced upward. The steep terrain now became his ally, offering him some cover and concealment.

"Nearing the crest of the bluff, the terrain becomes almost vertical and is almost twenty feet in height," said Dawson. "This afforded complete defilade from the entrenched enemy above. A machine-gun nest was busily firing at the beach, and one could hear rifle and mortar fire coming from the bluff crest." Dawson crept forward.

"I tossed two grenades aloft into the enemy trench, and upon exploding the machine-gun nest became silent. I waved my men and Spaulding to proceed as rapidly as possible, and I then proceeded to the crest where I saw the enemy moving out toward the E-3 exit and the dead Germans in the trenches."

Dawson was first to the top. His tiny attack made the first crack in the German line and compromised the defenses guarding the E-3 exit. To the west, the men in half-tracks attempted a second breach.

Sergeant Hyman Haas (467th AAA) landed with his two half-tracks directly in front of WN 65. "Down came the ramp," he said, "and we disembarked. It was nothing. The entire platoon lined up on the beach; there was pandemonium and firing. I could hear the German machine guns, and I was facing exit E-1, my objective.

"The beach was not in control. We were lined up one half-track after another—ten in all—and all of a sudden I found myself looking up a pillbox, dug directly into the cliffs. One of the officers on the beach, an infantry officer, immediately caught our attention and began pointing towards that pillbox. That only meant one thing—that it was alive and in action. None of the other half-tracks reacted, so I did."

Haas directed his vehicle (an M-15), with its 37mm cannon and two .50-caliber machine guns, back into the water and maneuvered it broadside to the fortified position. Had he placed his vehicle so the hood faced the enemy, he would not have been able to depress his guns to fire. So he engaged them from this broadside position. Meanwhile, the menacing gun in the concrete casemate blazed away.

The second vehicle, the M-16, with its deadly quad .50s, also drove back into the water, and took up a firing position just twenty-five feet from the M-15. The M-16 opened fire with the quad .50s, the guttural roar and blazing firepower welcome relief to the beleaguered soldiers. The fire covered the target. Haas then fired his 37mm cannon.

"I opened fire, and was hitting below the pillbox, whereas Hart [on the .50 caliber] was peppering the target. My first three shots were low. I took the antiaircraft range, and clicked that off, and raised the sights three clicks. The next ten shots went directly into the porthole of the pillbox.

"We fired one full clip and part of a second clip of 37mm ammunition, and they went directly into the pillbox and that was the end of that."

Widerstandsnest 65 became a beehive. The massed half-tracks answered the German fire. Adjacent to the 467th, the 197th AAA added the weight of its sixteen vehicles to the attack. PFC Al Sponheimer was with the medical detachment of Battery A.

"When we got on shore, everyone turned to the right and we lined up on the beach. We were lined on a hundred yards stretch, with sixteen half-tracks. We couldn't see out of the windshield because the steel plate was down, and the driver and the lieutenant could only see out of two slots in the front.

"When we stopped, all you could see was the ground just covered with dead GIs. You could hardly see sand. It was terrible. All we owned on that beach for the next four hours was about ten yards. When we finally did get out of the track, we tried to drag some of the bodies—from in front of the tracks, from underneath the vehicles—out of the water and bring them up where they wouldn't get washed back out to sea."

Two of the tracks backed out into the surf and turned around, presenting the rear of the vehicles to the cliff, and backed up the sloping beach. From that position, the multiple guns of the two vehicles delivered devastating fire on the high ground.

The 467th and 197th AAA had cleared the way in the center of Omaha Beach. Exit E-1 was open.

Al Sponheimer Jr. served in the medical detachment of Battery A, 197th AAA.

10

THE 116TH REGIMENT: INTO THE JAWS OF HELL

On the western half of Omaha Beach, the 116th Infantry Regiment of the 29th Division assaulted the Dog sectors labeled Green, White, and Red. The key objectives were the two exits off the beach at Vierville-sur-Mer and Les Moulins, labeled D-1 and D-3.

The first wave, scheduled to attack at 0630 on a line stretching from D-1 to D-3, consisted of Companies A, G, F, and E. Company E, on the extreme eastern flank, was to tie in with Company E of the 16th Regiment.

But the German mines and obstacles broke that line of advance as coxswains of the LCAs searched for openings through the deadly barricade. Company E of the 116th actually landed a half-mile off course through four gaps in the obstacles. Their men were intermingled with the men from Company E of the 16th.

Company F landed partially in its sector, but Company G actually landed to the right of F instead of to the left. Alone among the four assault companies, Company A plodded on, exactly on course, its coxswains guided by the most prominent landmark on the beach—the steeple of the Vierville church, right at the D-1 exit. Following in trace of Company A were Companies B and D, all bound for Dog Green sector of Omaha Beach.

 Disk 2, Tracks 18–22: The 116th Infantry at Omaha Beach

OPPOSITE: Troops disembark LCI 412 at Omaha Beach.

TIME LINE	Dec. 7, 1941	Jan. 15, 1944	June 4, 1944	June 5, 1944	JUNE 6, 1944	0015–0300	0530
	Japan attacks Pearl Harbor; American enlistments increase	Eisenhower becomes supreme commander; planning intensifies	Resistance operatives in France put on D-Day alert	Eisenhower makes decision to proceed with invasion		Airborne troops land in Normandy (British to the east, then Americans to the west)	Allies bomb beaches; first ground troops land on an island off Utah Beach

0630	0700	0730–0745	0930–1330	1203	1300	1600	2400
H-Hour on Utah and Omaha Beaches	U.S. Army Rangers scale Pointe du Hoc	H-Hour on Gold, Sword, and Juno Beaches	Troops advance inland	British commandos meet airborne troops at Orne bridges	U.S. 4th Infantry meets 101st Airborne at Pouppeville	Tanks move inland from Omaha Beach	Five beach-heads secured; liberation under way

John Barnes was aboard the sinking Boat #5, with other members of Company A.

But before Company A could even reach shore, there was trouble. One of its six boats (Boat #5) began filling with water and sank.

"Smoke clouded the lower coastline," said Private John Barnes, in Boat #5. "We could just see the bluffs, and above that, the single spire of the church; it was Vierville. We knew it. We were right on target.

"Our LCA roared ahead, buffeting the waves. Suddenly a swirl of water wrapped around my ankles, and the front of the craft dipped down. The water quickly reached my waist, and we shouted to the other boats on our side. They waved in return."

One man drowned and the rest floated helplessly in the water, out of the fight. Company A had lost one-sixth of its fighting force still a thousand yards from shore.

"When we got to the beach," said Sergeant Tom Valance, "the obstacles erected by the Germans to prevent the landing were fully in view as we were told they would be, which meant the tide was low."

The coxswain held the landing craft steady and dropped the ramp. The men of Company A jumped off into knee-deep water and began to move forward and then crouch to return enemy fire.

"There was a rather wide expanse of beach," said Valance, "and the Germans were not to be seen at all, but they were firing at us, rapidly, with a great deal of small-arm fire. One of the problems was we didn't quite know what to fire at. I saw some tracers coming from a concrete emplacement, which to me looked mammoth. There was no way I was going to knock out a German concrete emplacement with a .30-caliber rifle."

Valance was hit in the hand, but pushed forward. Then it seemed he was engulfed by German fire.

"I was hit again, once in the left thigh, which broke my hip bone, and a couple of times in my pack, and then my chin strap on my helmet was severed by a bullet. I worked my way up onto the beach, and staggered up against a wall, and collapsed there. The bodies of the other guys washed ashore, and I was one live body amongst many of my friends who were dead and, in many cases, blown to pieces."

DOUGLAS BRINKLEY AND RONALD J. DREZ

Troops stay low as their LCVP approaches Omaha Beach.

Company A was pulverized on the beach. The unseen guns were locked onto the killing zone of Dog Green sector. Two giant concrete bunkers were at the foot of D-1, both firing down the beach. High above those two massive positions was WN 73, dominating the long axis of the beach and almost invisible. Its 100-millimeter gun did not miss, and it hammered out deadly fire as fast as the gunners could shoot. From the top of the cliffs, the infantry of the German 352nd Division poured fire into the landing craft and disembarking troops.

Still the boats of the 116th Regiment came on like moths drawn to a flame. Their reward for perfect navigation to the correct landing beach was to enter into the jaws of hell.

Landing troops help a comrade whose ship went down offshore.

"The company commander was Captain Taylor N. Fellers and the exec was Lieutenant Ray Nance," said PFC George Roach. "Lieutenant Anderson headed up our thirty-man boat team.

"When we hit the sand, the ramp went down and Lieutenant Anderson was the first off the boat with Private Dominguez. In the next few seconds, I went off, and I saw Dominguez had already been shot and was lying in the water and sand. Lieutenant Anderson was twenty-five to thirty yards in front, waving his hand for us to move forward, and suddenly there was no more sign of life from him."

One of the other Company A boats did not land in shallow water. "The lieutenant ran off at the middle of the ramp," said PFC Gil Murdoch, "and was immediately cut down by machine gun fire and killed. Rodriguez, who was a private, ran off at the right side and he was immediately cut in half by machine gun fire. I jumped from the port side of the ramp and found myself in about nine feet of water. The landing craft had not landed on the beach, it had landed on a runnel, or a sandbar."

DOUGLAS BRINKLEY AND RONALD J. DREZ

The coxswain, realizing the error, backed off and came ahead again with the ramp lowered. Murdoch was hit by the ramp but managed to grab a rope on the port side as it went in. The LCVP dragged him to the beach from where he tried to crawl forward.

"I finally came under one of the underwater beach obstacles, which was out of the water and there were two men there. I spoke to them for a few moments and then I saw somebody crawling quickly backwards to us, and I saw it was George Roach with the flamethrower. I asked what happened and he said all of the officers were dead, and all of the noncoms were dead, and he and I, as PFCs, were the senior men on the beach as far as he could see."

Roach was right. The only surviving officer was First Lieutenant Ray Nance, the executive officer, and he was not yet on the beach.

"I went in with B Company, which actually was nineteen minutes after A Company," said Nance. "I was the first one off. It was a division order that an officer be the first man to go off the boat. When I got up there and dropped and I looked around in front and all around—I mean, not a soul. Nobody in front. Where was everybody? Where was A Company? I didn't know until I got in above high water what happened to A Company. I turned around and saw the bodies in the water—they were bumping against one another it was so thick. There was nobody in sight. I turned and looked, nobody in sight—nobody behind me."

Nance was alone on the beach. At the water's edge he spotted some men hunkered behind an obstacle.

"Four men from the 29th Recon were behind one of those steel jack things, and I yelled for them to scatter out, and no sooner than I said that, a mortar round came in and killed three of them and wounded the other. I saw Lieutenant Winkler of B Company; he was on my right and they were going down just like hay dropping before the scythe, just mown down, and Winkler was killed."

On came Company B. Down went the ramps, and the machine-gun fire entered the boats before the men could step off.

"The ramp went down and Captain Zappacosta was the first man off," said PFC Robert Sales, "and they just riddled him. It didn't kill him instantly, but he was hollering at me. Everybody

(From left to right) Lieutenants Ray Nance, Edward Gearing, and John Clements were in the ill-fated 116th Regiment at Omaha Beach. Nance, an executive officer who arrived with Company B, may have been the only officer to survive the initial landings of the 116th.

Part of Boat Team #5, Company A, 116th Regiment, is shown here in May 1944. Their boat sank on its way in to the Dog Green sector of Omaha Beach.

who went off, they just cut them down. We got caught in crossfire. The only thing that saved me, I stumbled and went off the side of that ramp. I looked back and as fast as everybody was coming off of that boat, they were just dropping. Zappacosta hollered to me that he was hit, and I started toward him, and he just went down and didn't come back up and I knew that was the end of him. We were cut to pieces. A, B, and D Companies, the ones that landed right there by those pillboxes by the Vierville draw were caught in a crossfire. Most of those men are in that cemetery there." Robert Sales was the sole survivor of his boat team.

PFC Harold Baumgarten came in on a sinking boat of Company B. The lieutenant had pressed his body against the ramp to slow down the onrush of seawater.

"Bullets were passing through the thin wooden sides of our vessel. The ramp was lowered, and the inner door was opened. In a British LCA we could only get out one at a time, and a German machine gun trained on the opening took a heavy toll of lives. Many of my thirty buddies went down as they left the LCA.

"Sergeant Barnes got shot down right in front of me, and Lieutenant Donaldson, and another sergeant had a gaping wound in the upper right corner of his forehead. He was walking crazily in the water, without his helmet, and then he got down on his knees and started praying with his rosary beads, and at that moment, the Germans cut him in half. The fire came from a pillbox built into the mountain on the right flank of the beach [WN 73]."

The German machine guns were zeroed on the small boats. Those few men who escaped the quick-fire guns still had to contend with the mortars and larger weapons raking the beach.

Company D followed Company B. The ramp went down and the machine guns answered. Sergeant Robert Slaughter, whose name had a special meaning on the beach, jumped off the side of the ramp into deep water.

"I could see some of the landing craft taking tremendous fire," he said. "After we got ashore, I looked back. Some of the people got hit and they were in the water bleeding, and I saw one man get tangled up in the motor of the landing craft. He was going around and around in that motor. As the landing craft

DOUGLAS BRINKLEY AND RONALD J. DREZ

started backing out with the ramp still down they took a hit. I don't know whether they hit one of the mines on the landing obstacles or what, but they took a hit and it sank."

George Kobe of Company D looked over the gunwales of his LCVP as he approached shore.

"We landed in the third wave, and as we went in, it was quite rough and the sea was choppy, but as we were getting closer to the shore it seemed to level out a little bit. We could see up ahead what was going on. Company A had hit the beach first and then B Company. Things didn't seem too bad from where we were, and Captain Shilling said, 'See, I told you it was going to be easy.'

"But when we went in, they threw everything at us. The Germans scored a direct hit on us and an 88 shell hit us, tearing off the ramp and knocking off both steel doors. Captain Shilling was hit and killed instantly by the steel door. The whole front of the LC was knocked off and the other door hit our platoon sergeant and knocked his left eye out."

To the east of Dog Green, the situation was almost as bad. At Dog Red, Sergeant Harry Bare landed.

"Company F assault boat landed on Dog Red Beach, further east than planned. Fire rained down on us, machine gun, rifle, rockets from the bunkers on top of the cliff. I saw assault boats like ours take direct hits. The men went over the sides of the boats to avoid the fire. The boats were zigzagging to avoid being hit. Our boat dropped its landing ramp somewhere near Les Moulins, and my lieutenant, the first off, took a shot in the throat, and I never saw him again.

"As ranking noncom, I tried to get my men off the boat, and make it somehow to the cliff, but it was horrible—men frozen in the sand, unable to move. My radioman had his head blown off three yards from me. The beach was covered with bodies, men with no legs, no arms—God, it was awful. It was absolutely terrible."

Toward the center of the beach, two of the larger LCIs came ashore. Each of the vessels had over 150 men aboard, plus cargos of reels of wire, satchel charges, Bangalore torpedoes, flamethrowers, grapnels, and other supporting matériel.

PFC Gilbert Murdoch landed with Company A.

A dead American soldier lies on Omaha Beach, one of thousands to perish in the assault.

"The front deck was crowded and we were beginning to get small-arms fire," said Lieutenant Robert Walker, aboard LCI 91. "I could hear some bullets hit the sides of the boat. An LCI has a pair of movable ramps alongside the bow, which would be lowered when the troops were to land. I was supposed to go down the ramp on the starboard side. As our boats moved into the lines of underwater obstacles, it seemed to get caught on one of the pilings which were slanted downward in the water toward the boat. The boat slid up on the piling and there was an explosion which tore the starboard landing ramp completely off the boat and threw it high into the air before it landed in the sea about twenty yards away."

The coxswain backed the craft off of the obstacle. Walker headed for the port side where the other ladder was intact but engulfed in flames. Small-arms fire raked the deck as the German gunners zeroed in on the range. Suddenly there was a blast and a soldier carrying a flamethrower erupted in flames, burning nearby companions.

DOUGLAS BRINKLEY AND RONALD J. DREZ

"The man with the flamethrower was screaming in agony as he ran over to the starboard side and dived into the sea," said Walker. "I could see that even the soles of his boots were on fire."

The captain signaled to abandon ship, and Walker climbed over the rail and dropped into the sea. He found himself swimming among the dead and dying, with mortar rounds trying to pick off those lucky to have survived. He swam in, alternately swimming, sinking, and gasping for breath. Waves foiled his attempts to stand and took their toll on his strength. Soon he began to jettison his gear in an attempt to survive.

"First, I dropped my rifle," he said. "Next came my helmet, and then the harness with the musette bag. With that much gone, I was able to swim the next hundred yards and touch bottom. Here I was on Omaha Beach. Instead of being a fierce, well-trained, fighting infantry man, I was an exhausted, almost helpless, unarmed survivor of a shipwreck."

LCI 92 was only a few yards to the left of the ill-fated LCI 91. It ran past with throttles wide-open, heading for the beach. But its fate was the same.

"Some few yards to the right of us, another LCI was drifting aimlessly riddled by 88s," said Yeoman Garwood Bacon Jr. "Machine-gun fire was mercilessly cutting to ribbons any floundering troops who had managed to jump clear of the smoking and burning hull. On our left along the obstacles, I could see two or three LCMs sunk or overturned.

"Suddenly a blast shook our sturdy little craft from stem to stern and a sheet of flame shot up thirty feet in the air through the #1 hold directly forward of the conning tower. A fire broke out below and smoke and flames poured out of the gaping hole. As if the explosion were a prearranged signal, the Jerries opened up with everything, and terror seized me as I gazed horrified at the burned and bleeding, frantically rushing and stumbling past me trying to get away from the blinding fire and smoke."

LCT 614 carried sixty-five men from the 116th Infantry Regiment and an assortment of bulldozers and jeeps and trailers. Ensign Donald Irwin was in command.

PFC Robert L. Sales was with Company B of the 116th Regiment. He was the sole survivor of his boat team.

PFC John Robert (Bob) Slaughter had been trained among the original 29th "Blue & Gray" Division at Fort Meade, Maryland. He was with Company D on D-Day.

"We finally dropped our ramp to get our troops and equipment off, and then all hell did tear loose. We came under intense fire, as did the LCTs to the right and left of us. Most of the fire seemed to be rifle, machine gun, and mortar fire. But I found I still couldn't get the soldiers and equipment off because the water was still too deep.

"A couple of bulldozers were driven off our ramp in pretty deep water, but did reach the shore, only to be blasted by German gunners with phosphorous shells which started them burning.

"Then some of the soldiers with a couple of the commissioned officers leading took off from the ramp in water up to their armpits with rifles held high over their heads, and headed for shore. As soon as a few more of the soldiers left the ramp, two of them got shot just as they stepped off. The rest of the troops refused to leave. I could in no way force human beings to step off the ramp into almost certain wounding or death. There were bodies floating in the water. It was evident the invasion force at Omaha Beach was taking a bad beating."

From the German perspective, however, the scene was similarly frightening. German Private Franz Rachmann from the 352nd Division was in combat for the first time, firing from his position from atop the cliffs.

"There was thousands of ships, and we could see landing boats of American troops. Then came thousands of men at one time, coming on land, and running over the beach. This is the first time I shoot on living men, and I go to the machine gun and I shoot, I shoot, I shoot! For each American I see fall, there came ten hundred other ones!"

The right flank of the Omaha Beach attack was shattered. The first three waves were now an ineffective fighting force. Landing craft bringing in the supporting artillery were sunk. The 111th Field Artillery Battalion, consisting of twelve howitzers, was destroyed. Before 0900, eleven of its twelve guns were on the bottom of the channel.

Additional landings on Omaha were delayed because of the pileup of men and equipment pinned down on the beach. The Germans had control of the high ground. Defeat of the

DOUGLAS BRINKLEY AND RONALD J. DREZ

American landing was a real possibility until there came an unexpected development.

At 0740, Companies A and B of the 2nd Ranger Battalion landed at Dog Green sector, and ten minutes later, the entire 5th Ranger Battalion landed to their left at Dog White sector. They reinforced the survivors of the 116th to form a formidable fighting force.

These Ranger reinforcements were available only because the attack at Pointe du Hoc had been delayed. Colonel Rudder's force, which had drifted off course, had lost time reaching the Pointe. Although that attack had been successful, the signal had come too late for the rest of 2nd Battalion and all of the 5th Battalion to follow in trace. Those units had initiated the alternate plan to land at Omaha Beach to attempt to take Pointe du Hoc from the rear in an attack along the coastal road.

"The British crews worked us in," said Captain John Raaen of the 5th Ranger Battalion. "We landed on the beach, the ramps went down, Sullivan was first out and I was second. As I rushed across the beach, I yelled to the men coming out behind me, pointing over to the right: 'Headquarters over here!'"

Raaen then turned to look back at the beach and saw men everywhere, spread across the beach, dead and dying, and men in the water hiding behind obstacles.

Ranger Don Nelson lay behind the stone wall and watched the mortars impact between him and the creeping water line.

"General Cota came trotting down the beach behind us looking for our colonel," said Nelson, "and he asked us 'Where's your commanding officer?' We pointed to the right and said 'Down there.' General Cota went on down and said 'Lead the way, Rangers.'

"We went over the seawall, and right there was a big row of concertina wire. The first thing we had to do was stick a Bangalore torpedo under that, and filter through that one little hole. We worked our way up to the little town of Vierville."

The Rangers attacked with elements of the 116th Regiment (mostly Company C) and by midmorning, they had broken the German stranglehold on the beach.

Colonel James Rudder led the Ranger force that reinforced surviving members of the 116th at Omaha Beach and ultimately made progress inland possible.

Chapter

11

THE BRITISH 2ND ARMY AT GOLD, JUNO, AND SWORD BEACHES

The British 50th Northumbrian Division assaulted Gold Beach to the east of the Americans at Omaha Beach. Twenty-five thousand men were scheduled to go ashore, and the first of the force touched down at 0730. The Underwater Demolitions Team (UDT) was in first, but the Germans directed their fire directly upon it, resulting in few lanes cleared of obstacles for the approaching landing craft.

The LCTs came in and unloaded British special tanks known as Hobart's Funnies. This special armor had the capacity to bridge small streams, flail the land with rotating chains to detonate mines, and lay mats capable of assisting vehicles across the beaches. The DD tanks were also part of the special armor.

The landing was not unscathed. Twenty of the LCTs had struck German obstacles with attached mines and suffered damage. Some men were lost with their tanks, and others were wounded and their equipment damaged. Overall, though, the Germans were not defending the beach heavily.

 Disk 2, Tracks 23–26: The British and Canadian beach invasions

OPPOSITE: Troops of the British 50th Division come ashore at Gold Beach, the farthest west of the three British-Canadian invasion beaches, and the one that offered the least resistance.

TIME LINE

Dec. 7, 1941
Japan attacks Pearl Harbor; American enlistments increase

Jan. 15, 1944
Eisenhower becomes supreme commander; planning intensifies

June 4, 1944
Resistance operatives in France put on D-Day alert

June 5, 1944
Eisenhower makes decision to proceed with invasion

JUNE 6, 1944

0015–0300
Airborne troops land in Normandy (British to the east, then Americans to the west)

0530
Allies bomb beaches; first ground troops land on an island off Utah Beach

0630	0700	**0730–0745**	0930–1330	1203	1300	1600	2400
H-Hour on Utah and Omaha Beaches	U.S. Army Rangers scale Pointe du Hoc	**H-Hour on Gold, Sword, and Juno Beaches**	Troops advance inland	British commandos meet airborne troops at Orne bridges	U.S. 4th Infantry meets 101st Airborne at Pouppeville	Tanks move inland from Omaha Beach	Five beach-heads secured; liberation under way

To Lieutenant Pat Blamey, who landed his Sherman tank on Gold Beach, it seemed more like a beach landing exercise than the long-awaited invasion.

"The only difference that there was were the LCTs blowing up on the beach obstacles and swinging about."

"The beach defenses on Gold Beach were not as numerous as I had been led to believe," said Lieutenant Brian T. Whinney, of the Royal Navy. Whinney was the Principal Beachmaster for Gold Beach. "I was able to conn the LCA, whose coxswain, a Royal Marine, did extremely well and avoided everything. We beached at about 0745 with a hundred to a hundred-fifty yards to run to the top of the beach. There was considerable gun and mortar fire, with resulting casualties, one of whom was the commanding officer of the Hampshires. I continued up the beach with our party who were then deployed along the beachhead."

Lieutenant Whinney observed a strange sight as he got to the top of the beach. The soldiers there were not fighting and in fact were sitting quietly, gazing out to sea as if on a holiday, watching the scene unfold before them.

"It took a few moments for me to realize that they were the Germans who'd been manning the beach defenses," he said. These soldiers were prisoners.

But while these soldiers were sitting, other German forces were not idle. On Green Beach, the westernmost beach, guns from a large pillbox enfiladed the landing area just east of Le Hamel. Mortar fire poured down onto the narrowing beach from the waterline to the sand dunes.

"I stopped the clearance of beach obstacles," said Whinney, "as no landing craft were beaching, and with the heavy surf and enemy fire, it was too great a risk for the personnel concerned."

The lieutenant spotted a mortar in operation and tried to knock it out. "I directed a corporal with a Bren gun onto one of the German mortar crews. It's a bit unnerving to see someone drop a bomb down a spout, knowing it is aimed in your direction."

The fire was effective and the mortar crew was forced to move. The pillbox continued to fire, but resistance on Gold Beach was still light.

DOUGLAS BRINKLEY AND RONALD J. DREZ

Seaman Ronald Seaborne was a forward observer for naval gunfire and landed almost unopposed. "By the time I was out of the water, there were two hundred or so troops already on the beach effectively dealing with the straggling rifle fire coming from the defenses of La Riviere on the eastern flank of Gold Sector," he said. "It was surprising that any of the defenders could have survived the preliminary battering from the rockets dispatched from LCT(R)s and the zebra-striped Sabres and Typhoons which I had witnessed during the run in."

Seaborne's shore-fire party, including a bombardier and a Royal Artillery captain, easily crossed the coastal road and then stopped to signal back to HMS *Belfast* that the beach was secure. But the captain moved ahead while Seaborne unsuccessfully attempted to signal *Belfast.* Eventually giving up and picking up his gear, Seaborne followed the captain's path only to find that he was alone.

"Suddenly, from a field ahead, emerged three men in German uniforms," said Seaborne. "This is the end of the war for me [I thought], but, as I went towards them, they raised their hands above their heads and by a mixture of French, German, and English, I understood from them that they were Russians who, after capture by the Germans, had been forced to act as members of a type of Pioneer Corps maintaining the Atlantic Wall. I showed them the way to the beach and waited until they were out of sight before proceeding."

The Royal Marines landing on the far right of Gold Beach found the going difficult because of obstacles, but the German resistance was feeble once they were ashore. Fifteen of their sixteen landing craft received some damage, but many men compared the landing to another practice exercise. There were only four hundred casualties among the twenty-five thousand men landed at Gold Beach, the least of any of the British invasion beaches.

The one German fortification that had been most troublesome for much of the day was finally silent as the German force pulled back. The beach was quiet and clear as the invasion force moved inland.

THE LANDING WAS NOT UNSCATHED. TWENTY OF THE LCTS HAD STRUCK GERMAN OBSTACLES WITH ATTACHED MINES AND SUFFERED DAMAGE. SOME MEN WERE LOST WITH THEIR TANKS, AND OTHERS WERE WOUNDED AND THEIR EQUIPMENT DAMAGED. OVERALL, THOUGH, THE GERMANS WERE NOT DEFENDING THE BEACH HEAVILY.

"Things quieted down during the afternoon," said Beachmaster Whinney, "and it was about 1700; I had met Colonel Phipps and all was quiet, but an eerie feeling remained, and not a soul in sight. We were about to return to the beach, when we heard a noise in a cottage. The colonel rapped on the door, and to our astonishment, an old lady appeared, and seemed quite unconcerned. She had apparently been there all day, carrying out her household chores as usual, although her house was backed onto the pillbox that had caused us so much trouble all day."

Meanwhile, the Canadian 3rd Division landed at Juno Beach. It experienced the same problem with the German obstacles as the British Royal Marines at Gold, only more so. The landing scheduled for 0745 was ten minutes late, delayed by offshore shoals, tricky tides and currents, and coxswains trying to pick their paths through the already submerged obstacles topped with mines. The mines took a heavy toll: almost 30 percent of the landing craft were destroyed or damaged before they even reached the beach. Company D of the Regina Rifles lost half its force before they could unload.

The German defensive force ashore watched the Canadians approach. There was little fire out to sea since most of the hardened, casemated positions, as at Omaha Beach, had been laid to deliver enfilade fire along the long axis of the beach. This deadly fire would engage the Canadians once they stepped ashore. Farther inland, the Germans had twenty batteries of artillery to support their small four-hundred-man force waiting to greet the Canadians.

Unlike at Omaha Beach, the defenders at Juno Beach did not have one-hundred-foot-high cliffs to dominate the beach. The defensive line was set in the beach houses and in the hardened positions along the beach.

Trouble began for the Canadians before the landing craft even got to the obstacles. Harvey Williamson, assigned to Headquarters Troop, DD Tanks, approached shore in an LCT with four other tanks. He was loaded in the rear of the craft and would go off last.

DOUGLAS BRINKLEY AND RONALD J. DREZ

Once the initial resistance was overcome, men and equipment began streaming ashore at the British and Canadian invasion beaches.

"When the first two tanks went off into the sea, they could then see that they were hundreds of yards from the beach, so they tried to reinflate. That took eighteen minutes. They blew up the screens and as they came up, the commander went around knocking the drags in so they could withstand the forces of the waves. These tanks were holding everything up, and the LCT had been hit. The naval commander ordered that tank to go down the ramp and it went straight to the bottom. The one behind got his screen up and took off, and was able to get away and make room for me to go off. I went into the sea, my propellers engaged, and I swam off to the shore."

The first tank ashore was a DD tank driven by Sergeant Gariepy of the Fort Garry Horse-10 Armored Regiment.

"More by accident than by design, I found myself the leading tank," said Gariepy. "The Germans opened up with machine guns, but when we came to a halt on the beach, they realized we were a tank when we pulled down our canvas skirt. Some of the machine gunners stood up in their posts looking at us with their mouths wide open. To see tanks coming out of the water shook them rigid."

Sergeant Gariepy identified the concrete position enfilading the beach. He drove forward with infantry following in his tracks.

THE GERMAN DEFENSIVE FORCE ASHORE WATCHED THE CANADIANS APPROACH. THERE WAS LITTLE FIRE OUT TO SEA SINCE MOST OF THE HARDENED, CASEMATED POSITIONS, AS AT OMAHA BEACH, HAD BEEN LAID TO DELIVER ENFILADE FIRE ALONG THE LONG AXIS OF THE BEACH.

The Germans from the houses peppered the beach, but the big blockhouse was stymied by the limitations of its own field of fire and Gariepy made sure that he stayed out of the killing zone.

"I took the tank up to the emplacement, very, very close, and destroyed the gun by firing at almost point-blank range."

"The first thing I saw going in was one landing craft being sunk," said Sergeant Stanley Dudka of the North Nova Scotia Highlanders. "There was a British soldier saluting as it was going down. He was standing on the bow.

"Our instructions were to break through—immediately hitting the beach—and to stop at nothing, not to fight unless we had to, but to get to Carpiquet Airport, and to consolidate Carpiquet Airport."

Lance Corporal J. H. Hamilton of the Third Battalion, Royal Winnipeg Rifles approached the beach in a damaged LCI. The LCI had been slammed back into the ship by the wave action as it was lowered into the water and one of the twin engines was damaged. The crippled LCI limped to shore as the waves threatened to sink the vessel.

"Because of lack of power, we were being swamped by heavy waves. The waves were so high, they were washing over our landing craft, and our first casualty was Rifleman Andrew G. Munch. He was very, very seasick. He was lying on the gunwale and the wave washed him off, and he went down. We never saw him again.

"We were being heavily fired upon approaching the coast. I was second in our section, and the lad in front of me was Rifleman Phillip Gianelli, and as the ramp went down, he took a burst of machine-gun fire in his stomach. He had been ahead of me. I wasn't touched by that burst. There was a tracer in it and you could see it coming to us—he was killed instantly." Hamilton crossed the beach only to be wounded himself, patched up, and wounded again and evacuated a month later.

The first wave of Canadians felt the full fury of the German defenses as they worked their way through the beach obstacles and into the killing field of the enfilading guns. Company B of the Royal Winnipeg Rifles was reduced to one officer and twenty-five men.

Among the most unusual equipment the British brought ashore were the specialized armored vehicles collectively known as "Hobart's Funnies." These included the flail tank, shown here, which was used to clear landmines.

Wilfred Bennett, with the Royal Winnipeg Rifles, landed in an LCA.

"Our commander was a good soldier. His name was Major Rupert Fultz of Winnipeg. The last order I heard from him as our ramp went down was 'OK boys, let's go.' We hit the water waist deep as all hell broke loose. Men were falling on the water, and they fell on the beach. The machine-gun fire was so devastating. A buddy, Kelly McTier, was on my right [and] was shot in the face and the neck."

Bennett struggled ashore carrying his rifle and a PIAT. A fellow soldier carried six bombs for it. A German pillbox delivered devastating fire on the Winnipeg Rifles and continued to cut the Canadians down until the pillbox was finally destroyed.

"After we crossed Juno Beach," said Bennett, "we took thirteen machine guns out of that pillbox, along with nine dead German soldiers. The Germans were using tracer bullets to direct their fire. As one bullet in five was a tracer, one can imagine how bullet-filled that beach was. As we crossed the beach, the fire was coming from a ten o'clock position and the air was yellow with tracer bullets."

> "THE FIRST THING I SAW GOING IN WAS ONE LANDING CRAFT BEING SUNK. THERE WAS A BRITISH SOLDIER SALUTING AS IT WAS GOING DOWN. HE WAS STANDING ON THE BOW."
>
> —SERGEANT STANLEY DUDKA

Bennett made it across, and once past the beach, the fire slackened. He moved into the town behind the beach, and although the fire was behind them, snipers picked at the invading troops. When they approached a small cemetery, a sniper opened up again.

"One trouble spot was an open gateway to a churchyard in Bernières-sur-Mer. We were having trouble getting past this area. I released one PIAT bomb into the belfry of that old stone church, blowing the back portion of the belfry away. We were able to proceed with little trouble from then on."

"There was tremendous congestion all along the beaches," said Sergeant Dudka. "To your left and to your right were troops landing at the same time and vehicles coming in. The roads were very narrow and very limited, and when we got ashore at Bernières-sur-Mer, we were held up there for approximately three hours."

By midmorning, the Canadians held Bernières-sur-Mer, and several hours later they occupied Saint Aubin. While they did not reach their ambitious goal to capture Carpiquet Airport, the Canadians did briefly interdict the Caen-Bayeaux road and linked up with the British 50th Division from Gold Beach.

But success had not been without cost. The Canadians had suffered 1,200 casualties out of the 21,400 attacking Juno Beach, a ratio equal to those grim statistics at Omaha Beach.

"Coming off the beach area, the narrow sandy beach," said J. H. Hamilton, "the first thing that really struck me was that there was a number of Canadian-Scottish that had been killed. They were laying about and the red poppies were in bloom then. It struck me then of a poem that we learned in school by McCrae: 'In Flanders fields the poppies blow / Between the crosses, row on row.' That certainly struck me when seeing the Canadian-Scottish laying dead amongst the red poppies blooming in the wind."

Sword Beach was the easternmost beach of the five Allied invasion beaches. Its left flank was at the mouth of the Orne River and the Caen Canal next to the town of Ouistreham. Its right flank, eight kilometers to the west, was the town of Lyon-sur-Mer. The entire area was dotted with vacation homes and tourist beach establishments behind a seawall.

Most important, Sword Beach was only nine miles north of the hub city of Caen. It was a key city for both the Allies and the Axis for maneuver and transportation. The German defenses could only be described as light, with beach obstacles and emplacements in the sand dunes.

The British 3rd Division assaulted Sword Beach at 0730, with French and British commandos attached. The objective was Caen. The attached commandos under Lord Lovat were to fight their way to the bridges seized at midnight by John Howard's glider-borne force.

The invading forces were greeted with moderate fire, but by 0800 many units were already off the beaches and fighting inland. The three assaulting regiments—South Lancashire on the right, Suffolk Regiment in the center, and East Yorkshire Regiment on the left—easily suppressed the German fire and pushed forward.

Entienne Robert Webb was in an LCA going in when it struck a German obstacle. "We caught one of those obstacles and it ripped the bottom of the craft like a tin can opener." Webb swam ashore. He was surprised to see that it did not look like a war at all.

"There was all this activity, bugles sounding, bagpipes playing, men dashing around, and commandos coming in off the landing craft and just moving off the beach as if it was a Sunday afternoon. There was no fighting on the beach, none at all. It was all inland."

Corporal Bill Bowdidge, Company D, Royal Warwickshire Regiment, had more trouble with his equipment than with the Germans. Caen was the objective, and Bowdidge was surprised to be given a bicycle.

"The original idea was D Company should cycle like mad behind the Sherman tanks into Caen. D Company members were called up on deck of the ship when C Company all had disembarked. Then they called on us to come up and unstrap the bikes, but not many bikes got ashore.

"It was difficult to get a bike down with the ramp hanging vertically, down in the deep water. We couldn't get our feet onto the beach while wearing a Mae West since the Mae West was taking my feet off the bottom, and [you] really had to sort of push with your

Sergeant Stanley Dudka of the Nova Scotia Highlanders attacked with the Canadian force at Juno Beach.

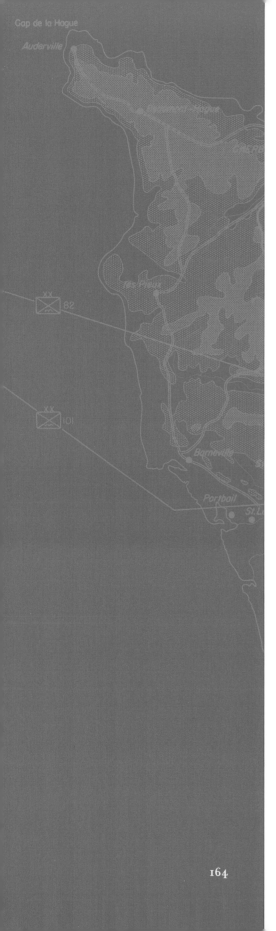

hands—paddle. I finally made it, and we were completely wet—absolutely soaked, and the beach was sandy, making it a difficult thing to get the bicycles ashore. I got mine ashore, somehow."

But instead of confronting German soldiers, Bowdidge was surprised to see a French girl helping with the wounded.

"The first French person I saw was actually on the beach. It was a young girl, seventeen or eighteen, with a bicycle, and she was helping casualties on the beach. She had on a homemade armband, a white armband, with a homemade painted red cross on it and she was making herself useful on the beach. It was quite extraordinary."

Corporal Bowdidge and the men of his section made their way to a rendezvous point, and found that of all the bicycles issued, only six or seven got ashore, and he was the only NCO with a bicycle.

"The company commander decided that I was going to have the bicycles, so he gave them all to my section. So instead of pedaling off down the road, we reverted to marching troops, and we set off cross-country, pushing the bicycles. We were right at the tail end of the company, hanging on and following them, not knowing where we were going.

"We didn't keep the bicycles formed for long after that, because we climbed over these cemetery walls, and then through a wood, and it was quite dense undergrowth in the wood, and we were having serious trouble keeping contact with the last man of the marching troops, so I just told my men to throw them away."

The girl on the beach was Jacqueline Noel, who had gone to the beach that day to retrieve a bathing suit she'd left in a bathhouse a week before. It was important to her since her sister, who was killed in an air raid, had given it to her. When she got to the beach, she could not turn back.

"I had the Red Cross thing since I was a student nurse, and I stayed there on the beach between Hermanville and Colleville, to help with the wounded and all the rest. I didn't go back to the house until two days after. There was a lot to do there.

"When I saw that invasion fleet, it was something which you just can't imagine if you haven't seen it. And it was boats,

Moving inland, British commandos would find armed resistance in the towns they aimed to liberate. Here the Number 4 Commando is engaged in house-to-house fighting in the town of Ouistreham.

boats, boats, and boats at the end, boats at the back, and the planes coming over. And you just—I mean, it had been—I don't know. If I had been a German, I would have looked at this, put my arms down, and said, that's it. Finished."

The commandos pushed off the beaches quickly. Peter Masters, normally of Number 3 Troop, 10th Commandos, was attached to 1 Troop, 6 Commando on D-Day. He had formerly been Peter Arany of Vienna, Austria, of Jewish extraction. In 1938 things under the Nazis had gotten so bad that his family tried to get out. Fourteen members were able to flee through the efforts of an aunt in London, the rest perished in Auschwitz.

Masters was attached to Captain Robinson's Number 1 Troop, which was a bicycle troop and promised to be the most active unit. As he headed down the ramp of his landing craft, he carried his rucksack, Tommy gun, two hundred spare rounds, and his bicycle.

"Our objective was Benoueville, and the bridges across the Orne Canal which were to have been seized by the paratroopers hours before. I carried two ropes to tow dinghies across the Orne should the bridges be blown. The order on which the

Peter Masters, born an Austrian, fought against Nazism as part of the British commandos.

greatest stress had been laid was 'Get off the beach.' And so we just moved up where there was a little dune. We walked across the dunes just off the sand part of the beach and passed a few fellows sweeping for mines, but we couldn't wait. We had been told to get off the beach and our Captain Robinson went right past them. They said, 'Hey, what are you doing?' But we said, 'Sorry about that, fellows. We've got to go.'"

Moving off of the beach, the commandos first worked their way through Ouistreham and the built-up area and then out into the countryside. The bridges were about three miles off the beach. When they got into the countryside, the terrain opened up and the troop was able to mount their bicycles.

After they had been riding the bicycles for a while, Robinson sent Masters alone into the village of La Port with orders to see what he could see. Although feeling much exposed, the young trooper walked toward the town, turning every so often to see his commander waving him on. He recalled a movie he had seen, *The Life of a Bengal Lancer*, with Errol Flynn and Cary Grant. Just before a superior force overwhelmed them, Grant uttered the line, "You're all under arrest."

"I always thought that to be quite a funny line," said Masters, "and it came to me at this precise moment. So I yelled at the top of my voice while I walked down the road, with my finger on the trigger of my tommy gun, 'Everybody out!' I shouted in German, 'Come out of it! Give yourselves up! The war is over for you! You don't have a chance unless you surrender now!' But I saw no one. No one came out."

Instead, a few Germans fired at Masters, who returned fire and was joined by Captain Robinson's charging troop and two tanks that made short work of the resistance. As the troop approached the vicinity of the bridges, Masters saw a white flag waving out of an upper window along with colored aerial recognition scarves. Some airborne men who had been isolated from their units trickled out of their hiding places to join the commandos. Although the bridges were only two hundred yards farther, no one could tell them the fate of Howard's force.

DOUGLAS BRINKLEY AND RONALD J. DREZ

The commandos moving inland would soon find the gliders of John Howard's force and link up with members of the British 6th Airborne Division who had landed earlier on D-Day.

"We turned the corner by the town hall," said Masters, "and there they were, and the maroon-bereted fellows gave a sigh of relief at the sight of our green berets. The feeling was mutual, for the bridges were intact. Gliders seemed to have crash-landed almost onto the bridges. On either side of the road, faces screamed their welcome from under maroon berets. For a while, the news almost kept up with our bicycles. 'The commandos have come,' said the glider people to no less relieved parachutists who popped out of the hedges in their camouflage all along the road."

The attack on Sword Beach was as successful as the American attack on Utah Beach. The flanks of the invasion area were secured. The British 3rd Division had landed over twenty-nine thousand men on D-Day with just over six hundred casualties. The commandos had linked up with the bridge force and although Caen was still six weeks from falling, this was a good start.

Chapter

12

THE AFTERMATH

As darkness fell on June 6, 1944, the invasion was successfully ashore. Almost 175,000 Allied soldiers had crossed the five beaches or jumped into the flanking parachute drop zones. There had been over 10,000 reported killed, wounded, and missing (many missing paratroopers later turned up). Despite the overall success of the day, the invasion force was vulnerable to German counterattack. Its lines were thin, with many gaps. In few places had the attack reached its objectives. General Eisenhower now faced the race to build up his landing force into a strong army capable of breaking out of the lodgment area.

In Paris that evening, many opinions were discussed in restaurants and meeting places, bars and salons. Members of the Resistance listened to the radio and conversations.

"The next morning came the official German special bulletin over the air," said Resistance fighter Henry Goldsmit. "'The Allies have made a landing attempt in Normandy. We have inflicted terrible casualties on them and are convinced that within twenty-four hours all their divisions will be eliminated. We are warning the population of France that any assistance to the enemy will be treated as a war crime and punished by death.'

 Disk 2, Tracks 27–29: Liberation and remembrance

OPPOSITE: A Coast Guard photographer found this monument to a fallen soldier, reminding all who saw it of the losses suffered in the invasion.

Dec. 7, 1941	Jan. 15, 1944	June 4, 1944	June 5, 1944	JUNE 6, 1944	0015–0300	0530
Japan attacks Pearl Harbor; American enlistments increase	Eisenhower becomes supreme commander; planning intensifies	Resistance operatives in France put on D-Day alert	Eisenhower makes decision to proceed with invasion		Airborne troops land in Normandy (British to the east, then Americans to the west)	Allies bomb beaches; first ground troops land on an island off Utah Beach

TIME LINE

0630	0700	0730–0745	0930–1330	1203	1300	1600	**2400**
H-Hour on Utah and Omaha Beaches	U.S. Army Rangers scale Pointe du Hoc	H-Hour on Gold, Sword, and Juno Beaches	Troops advance inland	British commandos meet airborne troops at Orne bridges	U.S. 4th Infantry meets 101st Airborne at Pouppeville	Tanks move inland from Omaha Beach	**Five beach-heads secured; liberation under way**

Dwight Eisenhower, Supreme Allied Commander, Allied Expeditionary Force, watches landing operations from the deck of a warship off the French coast. This picture is dated June 7, 1944. At this point, the Allies had secured the beachhead but were still vulnerable to an organized German counteroffensive.

"I made it my business to have my dinner that night in a German restaurant and listened to different opinions of the enlisted men. To my surprise I learned that the majority believed the military reports and were convinced that the Allies would not only fail in their invasion attempt but also that Hitler was ready to launch the *Wunderwaffe* on England and destroy the entire island within days. *Wunderwaffe* means the miracle weapon. I also took every opportunity to listen to the BBC, and heard an entirely different story. They sounded very optimistic and reported that in spite of some initial difficulties and casualties things were going according to plan."

The Allied attack had been a complete surprise. The Germans had been caught napping. They had misread the weather charts and made the wrong prediction; their high commander had gone on a holiday; their air force and navy had not shown up to attack the biggest target in the history of warfare, the armada. Although their intelligence and spy operation had cleverly identified the code words announcing the time of the attack and although the commander at Pas-de-Calais had reacted appropriately, the commander of the forces at Normandy had missed his great opportunity.

The Abwehr had been completely outwitted by the Allied intelligence, especially the British SOE and special agents, spinning tales of deceit and double-cross. The German command had been deceived into believing that Eisenhower had twice the strength that he actually possessed, and that the invasion would come at Pas-de-Calais. As D-Day came to an end the Allies were still telling their tantalizing tales.

Having hurled the massive invasion force a hundred miles across the English Channel in one throw of the dice, and having established a tentative foothold in France, Eisenhower now sought to perpetuate Operation Fortitude, the deception plan to conceal the secrets of the invasion. It became the task of Fortitude to continue to confuse the Germans regarding the significance of the Normandy attack.

Because of inflated numbers, the Germans believed the Allies capable of launching a second invasion when, in truth,

DOUGLAS BRINKLEY AND RONALD J. DREZ

Captured German officers aboard a
U.S. Coast Guard transport appear
relieved that their battle is over.

Operation Neptune/Overlord had no backup plan. It was all or
nothing for 1944. If the invasion failed it could not again be
attempted until 1945. And if the German Army could somehow
defeat the Allied forces that had scratched out a foothold on
June 6, that defeat would be worse than if the invasion had
failed at the water's edge.

Despite all of its failures and incompetence on D-Day, the
German Army still possessed the forces capable of inflicting a
last-minute defeat on the Allies. These were the massive
armored divisions within three days travel to the Normandy
battlefield. There were over sixteen hundred *panzers* in the
west that could be sent speeding to the battle area if Hitler
issued the order to "Initiate Case Three." If these forces could be
brought into the battle area from their dispersed positions in
France before the British and American forces could build up,
they were capable of delivering devastating blows on the flanks
and seams of the loose-knit Allied front.

After the battle, the Allies combed through equipment and documentation left behind by the Germans. Here members of the U.S. Navy 2nd Beach Battalion examine a radio-controlled "beetle" tank captured at Utah Beach.

To enhance the deception, the military and political leaders carefully chose their words to comment on the events of June 6. They couched their enthusiasm for D-Day in words designed to convey an anticipation of the great attack yet to come.

At 0917 on D-Day, Eisenhower's headquarters released the information announcing the landings. At 1000, the general was on the air announcing that the landings were an initial assault. The exiled leaders of Norway and Belgium followed, each emphasizing the initial attack at Normandy.

Even the rituals followed in Parliament in the House of Commons were not abandoned on June 6 to hint that this was the long-awaited day. In fact, just the opposite was true. In a display of calm and unruffled order that must have been maddening to all who had heard Eisenhower's announcement and were anxious for details, the House plodded painstakingly through its order of business.

After an opening prayer and some announcements, the House began with its customary hour of questions, mostly concerned with soldiers' rights, benefits, housing construction, and hours of employment in service canteens, etc. A lively debate even ensued concerning new berets for the women's army service, with one dissenter being rebuked by a supporter for his lack of gallantry in opposing the measure. The hour dragged on.

Finally at noon, Churchill entered the chamber and everyone moved to the edge of his seat, but still the prime minister played the nonchalant attitude to the fullest. He spoke first of the Allied success in the liberation of Rome two days earlier, then spoke for an agonizing ten minutes on the glorious event of United States' Fifth Army freeing the Eternal City.

After the ten minutes, he paused. His pause was longer than normal. When he began again it was to announce, almost offhandedly, that, "during the night and early hours of this morning, the first of a series of landings in force on the Continent of Europe has taken place . . . ." His speech ended with a statement about a "succession of surprises."

But how long could the deception last? Hitler had not initiated Case Three despite requests from Field Marshal Rundstedt commanding German forces in the west. He wanted to wait to see if a second Allied landing materialized before committing his reserves.

Finally, on the morning of June 8, the German High Command concluded, through captured documents, that this was the invasion, and Hitler initiated Case Three. Seventeen reserve divisions would now move to the Normandy battlefield. Hitler also ordered 360 tanks and thirty-five thousand men from the Ninth and Tenth SS Panzer Divisions in central Poland to move to Normandy, to arrive in the battle area in three weeks.

But the immediate threat to the Normandy beachhead was the set of forces moving from Pas-de-Calais. To counter that move, Eisenhower ordered an increase in the tempo of Fortitude message traffic, again to convince the Germans that Normandy was a diversion.

Real and dummy alert messages were now broadcast to Resistance groups just as had been done before the invasion. Around Dover, real and dummy ships and vehicles highlighted increased activity at the port. Agents such as "Garbo" (a code name) sent new message traffic feigning new revelations indicating that the real objective was Pas-de-Calais. The Allies cranked Fortitude up to the maximum. Double-agent message traffic was fed to the Germans reporting that high-ranking officials including Churchill, Eisenhower, and General George Marshall himself had visited General Patton's headquarters at Dover.

One agent reported five airborne divisions and ten seaborne divisions. Patton's army would have fifty divisions.

This crush of traffic, sightings, and reports of Allied movement was too seductive for the Germans to ignore. They predicted a probable second landing on June 10. The flood of information was fed to Adolf Hitler, who pondered it all and was himself convinced. At midnight on June 9, Hitler cancelled Case Three. Calais would be strengthened. The following day, the Allies

A U.S. Navy hospital corpsman takes a moment to write a letter from one of the Normandy beaches.

Allied troops moved inland after D-Day, liberating French towns and villages from their German occupiers. Here (in a rare film still) a group of American soldiers poses with a Nazi flag and sword they have captured.

consolidated their multilanding beachheads into a single front stretching sixty miles across the Normandy coast.

But despite canceling the movement of the forces at Calais, Hitler did have other units moving toward Normandy. Forces from the Riviera and Brittany were advancing. Especially troubling was the powerful Second SS Panzer Division, *Das Reich.* It consisted of twenty thousand battle-hardened veterans and 238 tanks and assault guns. It was stationed just outside of Montauban in the southwest of France.

Its route to the battle area was expected to take three days, and it became the target of British SOE, F Section, to attack and slow it down. Because of the shortage of fuel, *Das Reich* turned to the railroad to try to move its tanks. But the destruction and interdiction of the railroad had been a specialty of Anthony Brooks, code-named *"Pimento."*

Brooks had received his action message on June 5, *"Tetty laisse tic re tranquil,"* and had set about to stop all traffic on the rail lines between Toulouse and Montauban. The success of his clandestine sabotage on the rail lines and special

DOUGLAS BRINKLEY AND RONALD J. DREZ

railcars is borne out by the lack of transportation available to *Das Reich*.

"They started to move on the night of the 7th or early morning of the 8th," said Brooks. "They had half-tracks, which had lightweight guns, which they moved out almost immediately. But the tanks didn't start moving into Montauban marshaling yard before the morning of the 8th and then because the lines were blown and everything else, they tried to go off on to the flats, the few flats they had left. Then they abandoned those and tried various other ways, and they were back on the road in the Montauban area and going north out of the Montauban area by road on the 9th."

Brooks's job had been to "force the blighters on the roads," and force them he did. *Das Reich* was now subject to the delaying attacks of a dozen *maquis* and the deadly, strafing Allied aircraft on its route to Normandy.

"The rule was always: Make a violent attack with all your weapons on a constricted piece of road," said Morris Buckmaster, the head of F Section. "Don't get involved in long fighting. Do a mosquito attack—sting and sting again, but at a later time. Each group, as it completed its task of ambushing a party, went up further, and joined and strengthened the group ahead of them. They created a very great deal of havoc in the *panzer* division, and indeed, that *panzer* division never got into the Normandy fighting at all."

The *maquis* paid a huge price for their attacks by provoking crushing reprisals by *Das Reich*. But instead of three days, *Das Reich* arrived on the battlefield on D+17 (seventeen days past D-Day), too late to participate in the battle against the buildup of the Allied force. It also arrived minus scores of its *panzers* and had suffered an estimated four thousand casualties.

Once Eisenhower's armies secured their lodgment, the fate of the German Army was sealed. Securing that lodgment was a combination of planning, expertise, deception, and delaying attacks by the ruthless French *maquis* and other Resistance units. In all phases the Allies had trumped the German forces. Eleven months after D-Day, the Third Reich ceased to exist.

EPILOGUE

On the sixtieth anniversary of the Allied invasion of Normandy, a simple code word—D-Day—has become the prevailing symbol of American-style democracy prevailing over tyranny. And it has also become the name of a museum in New Orleans. Located near Lee Circle in the Central Business District (CBD), the National D-Day Museum tells the story of the more than 100,000 Allied soldiers swept ashore, and the nearly 10,000 who died, on the first brutal day of fighting. But World War II was not won on June 6, 1944, or even in the weeks immediately following. The visitor learns how by July 25 the Allies had broken out of Normandy and started on the long journey to Berlin. At the museum—in listening booths—you can hear the voices of our citizen soldiers: for example, men such as Felix Branhaur, who went ashore in the second wave at Omaha Beach as a demolition man for the 29th Division, or Dr. Bernard S. Feinberg, who as captain in the 116th Infantry served as the regimental dental surgeon. What is important to remember is that during the year following June 6, the valor continued.

But in any study of the historical dimensions of D-Day, one man's contributions outshine all the others. And he was not even officially in the U.S. military. Until the National D-Day Museum got under way, the name of Andrew Jackson Higgins had largely faded from American memory. Long ago this master boatbuilder and industrialist had been dismissed by his city's social elite as a crude, hard-drinking outsider lacking Old South manners and Garden District charm. But at the museum, his truly Herculean feat of building 20,094 boats for the Allied cause

DOUGLAS BRINKLEY AND RONALD J. DREZ

during World War II is not forgotten—nor is it forgotten by the veterans who stormed Normandy, liberated Sicily, fought on flyspeck Pacific Islands, or invaded North Africa.

The history of World War II often tends to focus on the leaders—admirals such as King and Nimitz, field generals such as Patton and Clark, strategists such as Marshall and Eisenhower. But World War II was not won only on the battlefield. Victory was made possible by industrial might and mobilization on the home front. Much has been written about the B-24 airplanes built in Henry Ford's eight-acre Willow Run Creek plant near Detroit, which Charles Lindbergh called the "Grand Canyon of the mechanized world." But it takes troops on the ground to win a war, and it was Higgins Industries in New Orleans that designed and produced the landing craft—LCPs, LCPLs, LCVPs, LCMs—that got them there.

To put Higgins's accomplishment in perspective, consider this: By September 1943, 12,964 of the United States Navy's 14,072 vessels had been designed by Higgins Industries. Put another way, 92 percent of the U.S. Navy was a Higgins navy. "Higgins's assembly line for small boats broke precedents," FDR's former adviser Raymond Moley wrote in *Newsweek* in 1943. "But it is Higgins himself who takes your breath away as much as his remarkable products and his fantastic ability to multiply his products at headlong speed. Higgins is an authentic master builder, with the kind of will power, brains, drive and daring that characterized the American empire builders of an earlier generation."

Who was this master builder? Born in 1886, and tossed of out of school for brawling, Higgins managed to complete three years at Creighton High Prep School before dropping out to join the National Guard. Drifting around the Gulf Coast states, he eventually landed a job in New Orleans in 1910 managing a lumber-exporting firm. Before long he organized his own business, the A.J. Higgins Lumber and Export Company, which sold pine planks and cypress blocks around the world. He also imported hardwoods from Central America, Africa, and the Philippines.

The roots of Higgins's wartime success lay in the fleet of schooners and brigantines he built to carry his lumber. In 1937 Higgins owned one little New Orleans boatyard where fifty or so people worked. By the time Japan bombed Pearl Harbor, he was designing prototype landing craft in a warehouse behind his St. Charles Avenue showroom and owned a massive boat-manufacturing plant in New Orleans. A perfectionist obsessed with good workmanship, he was also positioned to accelerate rapidly his shipyard production to produce shallow-draft watercraft, or even aircraft—whatever was needed. "The sad state of war," he said, "has made it my duty to build."

And build he did. Higgins Industries expanded into eight citywide plants, employing more than twenty thousand workers able to produce seven hundred boats a month. With a labor pool diminished by the numbers of young men enlisted or drafted, Higgins became an equal-opportunity employer by default, hiring women, blacks, the elderly, the handicapped—anyone he could find to build boats. Everyone who had the same job was paid the same wage. Together they set home front production records. Winning the Army-Navy "E"—the government's highest award for a company—was commonplace for Higgins Industries.

In his book *Andrew Jackson Higgins and the Boats That Won World War II,* historian Jerry E. Strahan recounts the frenetic boatbuilding mania that swept over the Port of New Orleans under the Higgins name. Higgins Industries constructed two kinds of military craft during the war: high-speed PT boats, and various types of steel-and-wood landing craft to transport fully armed troops, light tanks, and field artillery. It was this latter class of body that made the D-Day landing of June 6, 1944, feasible. "Without Higgins's uniquely designed craft," writes Strahan, "there could not have been a mass landing of troops and matériel on European shores or the beaches of the Pacific islands, at least not without a tremendously higher rate of Allied casualties."

No less an authority than General Eisenhower agreed. Higgins is "the man who won the war for us," he said. Ike's personal assistant Harry Butcher recalled his boss's saying in March 1943 that when he was buried, his "coffin should be in the shape of a landing craft, as they are practically killing [me] with worry." But a year later, because of Higgins Industries, there were enough LCVPs (or "Higgins Boats," as soldiers called them) for Ike to plan the D-Day invasion with one less worry. "Let us thank God for Higgins Industries' management and labor which has given us the landing boats with which to conduct our campaign," he told the nation that year in his Thanksgiving Day address. So crucial was Higgins's amphibious warfare craft that a disgruntled Adolf Hitler called him the "new Noah."

Andrew Jackson Higgins may have been short on social graces, but he was a production genius when his nation most needed him. His motto was "The Hell I Can't," and he always far exceeded expectations. The profane, no-nonsense Higgins uncomplainingly worked sixteen-hour days throughout the war. If he bitched about Washington bureaucrats, union leaders, foolish admirals, and New England shipbuilders, he never let down a U.S. soldier or sailor. There was no polish to his talk or elegance to his gait. He was a boatbuilder with a vision and the ability to turn that vision into reality. Higgins died in New Orleans in 1952, and Higgins Industries no longer exists, but there are many local old-timers who remember its enormous contributions to the Allied victory.

Higgins's genius is now receiving wider recognition, as predicted long ago by one contemporary who relied on him. "When the history of this war is finally written," Captain R. R. M. Emmett, who commanded landing forces in North Africa, wrote during the war, "by historians far enough removed from its present turmoil and clamor to be cool and impartial, I predict that they will place Mr. Higgins very high on the list of those who deserve the commendation and gratitude of all citizens." It took more than a half-century, but now, thanks to the remarkable exhibits at the National D-Day Museum, a great American boatbuilder and the workers he employed will never again be forgotten. Andrew Jackson Higgins is permanently enshrined as one of the most effective armorers in America's "arsenal of democracy."

ACKNOWLEDGMENTS

Over the years we have lectured to many about D-Day. Along the line we usually ask this question: What does the number 36,525 have to do with D-Day? The answers are many. Some guess that it was the number of ships, or planes, or soldiers, or enemy defenders, or casualties on that day in Normandy. Of course, all of those are incorrect. The number 36,525 refers to the number of days in each century. By nature, one of those days must rise above all others in importance. Who can argue that October 14, 1066 was "the" day of the eleventh century as the Battle of Hastings forever changed the course of western civilization? The eighteenth century's day was July 4, 1776, the day of the Declaration of Independence and the birth of the American nation, and a new cradle of freedom for people of the world. In the nineteenth century, July 3, 1863, the Battle of Gettysburg in Pennsylvania decided once and for all that the United States would remain one nation and not split into two.

The twentieth century produced a number of important dates: the end of World War I on June 28, 1919; the stock market crash on October 29, 1929; the announcement of the Salk vaccine for polio on April 12, 1955. But none of those dates can compare to the importance of June 6, 1944. It was "the" day of the twentieth century. It was the day of the beginning of the end to Adolf Hitler's Nazi terror that had gripped the people of Europe for eleven long years. This book is made possible by the Allied warriors who brought about the Nazi downfall and by those who were gracious enough to donate their stories so that the day will forever live in freedom's memory.

This book is dedicated to the indomitable Peter S. Kalikow, president of H. J. Kalikow & Co. Over the years his generous contributions to the Eisenhower Center for American Studies at the University of New Orleans allowed us to preserve the largest collection in existence of oral histories of D-Day and Battle of the Bulge veterans. In 2001 we named the entire collection the *Peter S. Kalikow World War II Oral History Project.* In New York circles, Kalikow's philanthropy is widely known. He is a stalwart champion of many worthy causes—and a true community leader. Currently a founding member of the board of trustees of the Museum of Jewish Heritage, he has proven his commitment to historical and cultural preservation. Alongside his many awards and civic accomplishments, Kalikow's efforts made this book possible. As well, his kindness and goodwill have perpetuated the historical endeavors of the Eisenhower Center for years to come.

In 2002 the Eisenhower Center for American Studies at the University of New Orleans transferred its monumental World War II archive to the National D-Day Museum. The Museum's president and CEO, Gordon H. "Nick" Mueller, is the enduring spirit behind the new institution. If honorary medals were to be given out to individuals who reminded American people about the selfless accomplishments of the Greatest Generation, Nick would receive the first one. Nick's vision to make the Museum a reality began years ago as a professor of history at the University of New Orleans. Working in partnership with Stephen E. Ambrose (as both friend and colleague), he never lost the faith. His enduring leadership has made the National D-Day Museum a colossal success, with over a million visitors since its grand opening on June 6, 2000. Nick has made the Museum's mission come true.

Without the continued work of Research Historian Marty Morgan and Assistant Research Historian Betsy Loren Plum at the National D-Day Museum, numerous voices of valor would be lost in time and irretrievable for students, scholars, and historians in the future. Museum Vice President of Development Hugh Ambrose has been involved with the oral history project since inception. Early on, his scholarly passion for capturing the stories of our veterans helped make the *Peter S. Kalikow World War II Oral History Project* possible. The Museum is proud of its dedicated Board of Directors: Herschel L. Abbott Jr., Richard Adkerson, Reuben V. Anderson, James Barksdale, Kenneth E. Behring, Tom Benson, Corinne Claiborne "Lindy" Boggs, Donald T. Bollinger, Frank Borman, Harold J. Bouillion, Philip J. Carroll Jr., Jacquelyn B. Clarkson, Harlan Crow, Robert C. Cudd III, Arthur Q. Davis, Alton F. Doody Jr., Ph.D., Anthony Drexel "Tony" Duke, Timothy C. Forbes, Alan I. Franco, Louis McDaniel Freeman Sr., Alexis Herman, Susan O. Hess, Marvin L. "Buddy" Jacobs, Peter Kalikow, Kenneth L. Klothen, David M. Knott, John E. Kushner, J. Wayne Leonard, James E. Livingston, USMC (Ret), E. Ralph Lupin, Commodore Thomas J. Lupo, Gordon H. Mueller, Gregory M. St. L. O'Brien, Thomas P. O'Neill III, Marc J. Pachter, Richard A. Pattarozzi, Philip Satre, George Shinn, Ted G. Solomon, Frank B. Stewart Jr., David R. Voelker, Virginia Eason Weinmann, Bruce N. Whitman, Pete B. Wilson.

DOUGLAS BRINKLEY AND RONALD J. DREZ

Thanks to the Eisenhower Center staff: Kevin Willey, Assistant Director, who held the fort during the concurrent activities; Lisa Weisdorffer, Project Coordinator, and Andrew Travers, Research Associate, for their tireless efforts in manuscript preparation; and in particular, Michael Edwards, Research Associate, for his invaluable and intimate knowledge of the tapes and transcriptions used in this manuscript. They have helped to carefully organize thousands of stories, oral histories, memoirs, letters, and photographs. In a time of change at the University of New Orleans, we welcome and embrace our new academic leaders. We are especially grateful for the support from Chancellor Emeritus Gregory O'Brien, and look forward to a grand future under the leadership of Chancellor Timothy P. Ryan. Special thanks to our former Provost, Louis V. Paradise, and his able and worthy successor, Rick Barton. And, as always, Robert L. Dupont, Dean of Metropolitan College and Vice Chancellor for Strategic Planning and Budget, who makes all of our projects come true.

The assembly and organization of a book such as this only come about through the coordinated efforts of many talented people. At becker&mayer! we would like to thank editor Ben Raker for always keeping this project together, from beginning to end; designer Todd Bates for contributing a sharp layout and cover; Shayna Ian for tracking down both personal and archival images; Kate Hall for solid sound-editing; Cindy Lashley for shepherding the book through its production; and Sheila Kamuda for overseeing the project. Thanks are due to becker&mayer! president Andy Mayer for placing it with its publisher. At Bulfinch Press, executive editor Michael Sand, with his belief in the book from the beginning and his sound editorial advice, and publisher Jill Cohen, with her commitment to publishing the finest illustrated books, recognized the merit of this project from the outset. Mr. Sand, along with assistant Eveline Chao, offered valuable suggestions and logistical assistance. Matthew Ballast, who makes sure the word gets out, oversaw the extensive publicity efforts. We are grateful to Stephen Lang for contributing crisp audio narration and introductions, which were recorded at the Kessler Media Studio in New York. The entire team at Bulfinch Press and Time Warner Book Group has been a pleasure to work with.

A special thanks to Judy Drez and the four Drez siblings who worked as willing assistants and cameramen during the years of research on the Normandy project. Finally, we would like to salute the founder of the Eisenhower Center and the National D-Day Museum, the late Stephen E. Ambrose, along with all those who worked on collecting and preserving the oral histories and memoirs of the World War II veterans.

Douglas Brinkley
Ronald J. Drez

GLOSSARY

AA: antiaircraft (antiaircraft fire or an antiaircraft weapon)

AAA: Anti-Aircraft Artillery (as in "Anti-Aircraft Artillery battalion")

Abwehr: German military intelligence

ack-ack: antiaircraft

Atlantic Wall: the German defense fortifications along the Atlantic coast of Europe

barrage balloon: a suspended balloon used to support a cable that prevented bombing aircraft from flying low over targets

bazooka: a hand-carried rocket launcher

Belgian Gates: barricade-like underwater obstacles

Case Three: the order for the German counterattack, issued only after long delay by Adolf Hitler

CO: Commanding Officer

commando: a specially trained assault troop

concertina wire: rolled barbed wire used to create an obstacle

COSSAC: Chief of Staff to the Supreme Allied Commander

dan buoy: a buoy used to mark the boundary of an area clear of mines or some other reference point

Das Reich: German Second S.S. Panzer Division (tanks)

davit: a small crane on a ship used to lower and lift small boats and materials into or out of the water

DD: Duplex Drive (characteristic of an amphibious tank)

D-Day: the first day of any military operation, most commonly used to refer to the day Operation Overlord launched

DSC: Distinguished Service Cross (a U.S. Army decoration for exceptional heroism in combat or in the British Navy for gallantry in action)

DUKW: an amphibious vehicle (a 2.5-ton truck)

DZ: drop zone (for paratroopers)

E-boat: a German torpedo boat

ECB: Engineer Combat Battalion

enfilade: gunfire or direction of fire from a flanking position along the long axis of an enemy line

ESB: Engineer Special Brigade

ETO: European Theater of Operations

FA: Field Artillery

FAB: Field Artillery Battalion

flak: antiaircraft fire

FUSAG: First United States Army Group

Gammon grenade: A weapon consisting of plastic explosive in a cloth bag with a strap; the user armed the explosive by holding on to the strap as the grenade was thrown

hedgehog: a portable obstacle consisting of three angled iron bars

Hobart's Funnies: a set of mechanized tanks designed specially for the D-Day invasion (swimming tanks, flail tanks, etc.)

IP: Initial Point (point of entry by air into an attack area; position near landing area where airborne troop carriers made final adjustments to their course)

LCA: Landing Craft, Assault

LCC: Landing Craft, Control

LCG: Landing Craft, Gun

LCI: Landing Craft, Infantry

LCM: Landing Craft, Mechanized

LCP: Landing Craft, Personnel

LCP(L): Landing Craft, Personnel, Large

LCT: Landing Craft, Tank

LCT(R): Landing Craft, Tank (Rocket)

LCVP: Landing Craft, Vehicles and Personnel

LSH: Landing Ship, Headquarters

LST: Landing Ship, Tank

Luftwaffe: the German air force

maquis: a guerrilla cell (or cells) of the French Resistance

maquisard: a member of a *maquis*

NCO: Noncommissioned Officer

OB West: *Oberbefehlshaber West*, the main German headquarters for the Western Front

Oberfeldwebel: German staff sergeant

Oil Plan: Allied plan to bomb German oil resources prior to the D-Day invasion

Operation Deadstick: the airborne training exercise involving the Ox and Bucks glider force

Operation Double Cross: an Allied intelligence effort to turn enemy agents and create false information

Operation Fortitude: the Allied deception plan to conceal the secrets of the Normandy invasion

Operation Neptune: the Allied plan for the cross-channel attack on D-Day

Operation Overlord: the Allied invasion of Normandy on D-Day

OSS: Office of Strategic Services

Ox and Bucks: Company D, Oxfordshire and Buckinghamshire Light Infantry Regiment (British)

panzer: a German tank

PC: Patrol Craft

PCC: Primary Control Craft

PIAT: Projector Infantry Anti-Tank (a handheld antitank weapon)

PIR: Parachute Infantry Regiment

Plan Tortue: Resistance plan to block roads

Plan Vert: Resistance plan to damage railway operations

Rangers: specially trained American assault troops

réseau: a French Resistance cell

SAC: Supreme Allied Command

SAS: Special Air Service

SHAEF: Supreme Headquarters, Allied Expeditionary Force

Silver Star: A U.S. military decoration for gallantry in action

SOE: Special Operations Executive

SS: German *Schutzstaffel* ("protection echelon"), a Nazi unit originally formed to protect Adolf Hitler and later expanded to achieve various functions of the Nazi party

Sten gun: a 9mm automatic rifle

TCS: Troop Carrier Squadron

Teller mine: a German antitank mine

Tiger tank: a heavy German tank

Transportation Plan: The Allied effort to bomb German transportation facilities before the D-Day invasion

UDT: Underwater Demolitions Team

WN: *Widerstandsnest* (a German "resistance nest" or fortified defensive position)

Wunderwaffe: A "miracle weapon" rumored to be possessed by the Nazis

PHOTO CREDITS

Key

NARA: National Archives and Records Administration
LOC: Library of Congress
IWM: Imperial War Museum
EC: The Eisenhower Center for American Studies
    at the University of New Orleans
USAMHI: U.S. Army Military History Institute

Endsheets: map: Department of the Army
Page 3: two soldiers: NARA
Page 7: troops line up for supplies: NARA
Pages 14–15: map of the Normandy invasion
    area: Department of the Army
Page 17: enlistment line: ©Bettmann/CORBIS
Page 18: Hearing Roosevelt's speech on radio:
    AP/Wide World Photos
Page 19: Army recruitment poster: ©CORBIS
Page 21: Fred Patheiger, courtesy of Denise Cox
Page 22: British citizens: IWM
Page 24: Harold Baumgarten, courtesy of
    Harold Baumgarten
Page 25: John Robertson, courtesy of John
    Robertson/EC
Page 26: training in Woolacombe: NARA
Page 27: Harry Parley, courtesy of Harry Parley
Page 28: LST blown apart by German E-boat: NARA
Page 31: Churchill, Roosevelt, and others: NARA
Page 33: Eisenhower, Montgomery, and soldiers:
    ©Bettmann/CORBIS
Page 36: William Tucker, courtesy of William
    Tucker/EC
Page 37: replica Sherman tank: The Tank
    Museum, Bovington (U.K.)
Page 38: Ed Jeziorski, courtesy of Ed Jeziorski/EC
Page 39: Joseph Blaylock, courtesy of Opal
    Blaylock
Page 40: troops board: Hulton Archive/Getty
    Images
Page 43: LST: NARA
Page 44: Rommel on the beach: NARA
Page 47: French Resistance fighters: AP/Wide
    World Photos
Page 49: railway bombing: copyright unknown

Page 51: Germans on railcars: AP/Wide World
    Photos
Page 52: Tiger tank: The Tank Museum,
    Bovington (U.K.)
Page 54: Rommel and men: AP/Wide World
    Photos
Page 57: German guard: AP/Wide World Photos
Page 59: British troops receive instruction:
    AP/Wide World Photos
Page 60: Richard "Windy" Gale: IWM
Page 63: John Howard, courtesy of EC
Page 65: Brian Priday, Ox and Bucks, courtesy of EC
Page 67: Howard and Wallwork beside the glider,
    courtesy of Kirt Garcia
Page 69: Jack Bailey and Wally Parr, courtesy of
    Kirt Garcia
Page 73: Pegasus Bridge: IWM
Page 75: parachutes dropping: NARA
Page 76: paratrooper getting in plane:
    U.S. Signal Corps
Page 77: paratroopers face-painting: U.S. Signal
    Corps (film still)
Page 78: Eisenhower with paratroopers: U.S.
    Signal Corps
Page 80: paratroopers in plane: U.S. Signal Corps
Page 81: Sidney Ulan, courtesy of Sidney Ulan
Page 82: camouflaged parachutes, courtesy of
    Carl Cartledge
Page 83: Dwayne Burns, courtesy of Dwayne
    Burns
Page 84: Carl Cartledge, courtesy of Carl
    Cartledge
Page 87: Dwayne Burns in gear, courtesy of
    Dwayne Burns
Page 89: paratroopers in jeep, courtesy of
    Denise Cox
Page 91: nighttime sea battle: U.S. Coast Guard
Page 92: B-26 bomber: NARA
Page 93: Alfred H. Corry, courtesy of Merle Corry
Page 94: 556th squad, courtesy of Merle Corry
Page 95: John Robinson, courtesy of John
    Robinson
Page 96: John (J. K.) Havener, courtesy of John K.
    Havener
Page 97: William J. Moriarity, courtesy of William
    J. Moriarity/EC

Page 98: loading in landing craft: ©CORBIS
Page 101: USS *Nevada* guns: NARA
Page 103: troops on an LCT: NARA
Page 104: general descending to boat: ©CORBIS
Page 105: USS *Arkansas*: NARA
Page 106: boat on fire: U.S. Coast Guard
Page 107: Sam Grundfast, courtesy of Sam
  Grundfast/EC
Page 108: German mine exploding: U.S. Coast
  Guard
Page 109: Malvin R. Pike, courtesy of Malvin R.
  Pike/EC
Page 110: troops on dunes: U.S. Signal Corps
Page 113: Utah Beach walls: NARA
Page 114: Don Malarkey, courtesy of Don
  Malarkey/EC
Page 117: A-20 bombers: NARA
Page 118: U.S. Rangers in an LCA: NARA
Page 119: James Eikner, courtesy of James Eikner
Page 120: Donald Scribner, courtesy of Mary
  Scribner
Page 121: climbing rope up cliff: NARA
Page 122: Sidney Salomon, courtesy of Sidney
  Salomon
Page 123: Ralph Goranson, courtesy of Carol Mount
Page 124: beach craters: USAMHI
Page 125: Leonard G. Lomell, courtesy of Leonard
  G. Lomell
Page 126: German fortifications: NARA
Page 127: Sidney Salomon getting silver star,
  courtesy of Sidney Salomon
Page 129: wading to the beach: NARA
Page 130: Omaha Beach map: Department
  of the Army
Page 131: Franz Gockel, courtesy of Franz
  Gockel/EC
Page 132: pinned down at Omaha Beach: Robert
  Capa © 2001 by Cornell Capa/MAGNUM
Page 133: Robert H. Miller, courtesy of Robert H.
  Miller/EC
Page 134: Jerry W. Eades, courtesy of Jerry W.
  Eades/EC
Page 135: German gun emplacement: U.S. Signal
  Corps
Page 136: beach obstacles: NARA
Page 138: men under ledge: U.S. Signal Corps
Page 139: Steve Kellman, courtesy of Steve
  Kellman/EC
Page 140: Hyman Haas, courtesy of Hyman
  Haas/EC

Page 141: Albert Sponheimer Jr., courtesy of
  Albert Sponheimer Jr.
Page 143: LCI headed to Omaha Beach: NARA
Page 144: John Barnes, courtesy of John Barnes
Page 145: troops in LCVP: NARA
Page 146: helping soldier from water:
  U.S. Signal Corps
Page 147: Ray Nance and others, courtesy of
  John Barnes
Page 148: Boat Team #5, courtesy of John Barnes
Page 149: Gilbert Murdoch, courtesy of
  Gilbert Murdoch/EC
Page 150: dead soldier: NARA
Page 151: Robert L. Sales, courtesy of
  Robert L. Sales/EC
Page 152: Bob Slaughter, courtesy of
  John Robert (Bob) Slaughter/EC
Page 153: Colonel James Rudder: USAMHI
Page 155: bikes unloaded at Gold Beach: IWM
Page 159: troops unload at Sword Beach: IWM
Page 161: flail tank: IWM
Page 163: Stanley Dudka, courtesy of
  Stanley Dudka/EC
Page 165: commandos in Ouistreham: IWM
Page 166: Peter Masters, courtesy of
  Peter Masters
Page 167: crashed gliders: courtesy of Kirt Garcia
Page 169: memorial: U.S. Coast Guard
Page 170: Eisenhower: U.S. Signal Corps
Page 171: German officers: U.S. Coast Guard
Page 172: captured "beetle tank": NARA
Page 173: soldier writing letter: NARA
Page 174: captured Nazi flag: U.S. Signal Corps
  (film still)

Cap de la Hague

Auderville

Beaumont-Hague

CHERBOURG

Fermanville

Barfleur

St. Vaast - la Hougue

les Pieux

XX 82

Valognes

Quinéville

Montebourg

XXX VII

Iles St. Marcouf

XX 4

les Dunes de Varreville

Douve R.

Merderet R.

XX 101

Ste. Mère-Eglise

UTAH

Barneville

St. Sauveur-le-Vicomte

Bancs du Grand Vey

Portbail

St. Lô-d'Ourville

St. Sauveur-de-Pierre-Pont

les Marécageuses

Carentan

Isigny

la Haye-du-Puits

Lessay

St. Jean-de-Day

Aire?

Périers

Taute R.

Vire R.

B   O

Villiers-Fossard

ST. LÔ

Coutances